SUCCESSFUL
WRITING

SUCCESSFUL WRITING

A Guide to Authors of Non-Fiction Books and Articles

GEORGE RYLEY SCOTT
F. Ph. S. (Eng.), F.Z.S.

The 'Successful' Series

1992

Lloyd Cole

Maidenhead

First Published 1943
Reprinted with amendments 1992

Lloyd Cole
37 College Avenue
Maidenhead, SL6 6AZ, UK

© Lloyd Cole, 1992

ISBN 1 874052 02 6

British Library Cataloguing in Publication Data
is available from the British Library

Produced for Lloyd Cole by
Chase Production Services, Chipping Norton, Oxon OX7 5QR
Printed in Finland

CONTENTS

PREFACE

When I first dabbled in journalism, the literary aspirant had not so many opportunities for securing help, advice and criticism as he has today. In my own case, I blundered along without any help or advice at all. I made, I suppose, every mistake it was possible to make. I wasted thousands of hours working along wrong lines. I chased scores of will-o'-the-wisps. In short, I served my apprenticeship in that roughest, hardest and most expensive of all schools – the school of actual experience. Looking back now, I wonder greatly how, in the face of the enormous difficulties and obstacles which beset my path, but of which, fortunately perhaps, at the time, I was blissfully ignorant, I ever managed to win through. And I have no doubt there are scores of other professional writers of twenty or more years' standing who, when they look back upon their early struggles, marvel much as I do.

In my opinion, the present-day literary aspirant is in many ways a much more fortunate individual than was his forerunner of a generation or so ago. He starts in the race with many advantages, not the least of which is the opportunity for securing advice and assistance which is presented today. In this way is he enabled to avoid a number of pitfalls which, in previous generations, delayed considerably the progress of almost every beginner, and in a big percentage of cases extinguished all hope at the very outset.

My own flounderings stand out big in my memory. I have very clear ideas as to the difficulties which troubled me, of the errors I made, of the time I wasted. There were, in those days, I well remember, many things which puzzled me greatly, many questions to which I would have liked authoritative answers. It is in an effort to answer these very questions and to assist the beginner in the solution of some, at any rate, of the problems which bother him, that I have ventured to make yet another addition to the already bulging shelves apportioned to handbooks for the edification and enlightenment of literary aspirants.

The scope and likewise the limitations of this particular book are indicated in the title and sub-title. The volume aims at covering the whole non-fiction field. It does not attempt to deal with the writing of short-stories and novels. The confection of fiction is an art in itself requiring a book devoted solely and exclusively to this art. More and further, this book deals solely with the craft of *writing for money*. It is not concerned, except incidentally and within definitely prescribed limits, with literary art *per se*.

There is a saying in circles where writers and their disciples forgather, that the main qualification required by the writer of a book on authorship is the failure to get his own scribblings published. In my own particular case, to prevent any erroneous classification, and to save the reader the trouble of consulting works of reference which may not be readily available, a word as to my fitness for the writing of this particular book is advisable.

Well, it is not a *first* book. Far from it. My published works, at the moment of writing, number 34. Most of my last thirty-five years have been spent, partially or wholly, in adding to the store of the world's literary matter. During this period, under my own name and under various pseudonyms, I have written hundreds of articles for all kinds of English, American, and (on occasion) foreign periodicals, ranging from literary essays appearing in the pages of such highbrow journals as *The New Age, American Speech,* and *The New English Weekly*; sociological articles for *Critic and Guide, The Freethinker,* and *Medical World*; to contributions to a miscellany of technical and trade journals, house organs, *et al*.

This short review of my literary career indicates the justification for a practical guide which is intended to give the results of a long and varied experience in the writing of articles and books. Despite the fact that there would appear, if sheer number is anything to go by, to be enough books, in all conscience, devoted to the art of writing, I am optimistic or egotistic enough to think that the result of this extensive experience will prove of use to beginners.

In the writing of the book I have assumed that the reader has a working acquaintance with the fundamental principles of English grammar and composition. This much granted, it is written and designed as a complete course of self-instruction for the student who wishes to teach himself all that is teachable in connection with the craft of the non-fiction writer.

George Ryley Scott
Cambridge

PART I

THE WRITER'S APPRENTICESHIP

1

SOME PRELIMINARY HOMETRUTHS

Can I become a successful writer? It is a question that a thousand persons are asking themselves every mortal day. For nearly everyone, at one period or another, is obsessed with a fierce desire to get into print. This desire may be expressed or unexpressed, it may be publicly denied even, but it exists nevertheless. Anyone who has had the privilege of seeing the piles of manuscripts which litter the editorial table of every popular periodical in London, knows the truth of this.

Why this itch for writing? Why this huge and ever-growing army of aspirants to journalism and authorship? Why these thousands of sweating scribblers?

In the 1930s the number of books published in the United Kingdom was about 15,000 per annum. By 1990 the number has risen to over 50,000. It is a stupendous figure.

The reason for the assiduity with which editors and publishers are bombarded with manuscripts are many, but the most important of them are: (1) the stories circulated of huge fortunes made by authors; (2) the fame associated with authorship; (3) the notion that a writer is a person of vast superiority; (4) the fact that authorship is one of the few professions that can be attempted with little capital and, according to the popular viewpoint, without an expensive or a prolonged apprenticeship; (5) the general idea that anyone who can write a long rambling letter is a born writer, and that to the born writer the task of authorship is a supremely easy matter. Let us examine these points seriatim.

In the first place, the rewards of authorship, so far as the public is concerned, are based upon the statements (often exaggerated) respecting the earnings of 'best-seller' novelists.

What is rarely mentioned either in the Press or in those alluring advertisements emanating from some of the schools which claim to be able to turn every schoolboy or servant girl into a successful author, is that, on an average, *only one book out of every fifty volumes published, whether it be a novel or a non-fiction work, earns for its author more than £1000*. Many earn much less than this, and as regards a considerable proportion of first books, and especially first novels, in each case the total royalty that rewards the author for six months' and possibly a year's work, is under £200.

Apart from exceptional cases, a non-fiction book by an unknown author offers much better prospects of financial success than does a novel. It is not anything like so much of a gamble, the publisher being in a position to gauge its selling prospects so much more surely. Moreover, it is not so likely to be still-born. And again it has usually a much longer life than any ordinary novel. Apart from reminiscences, autobiographies, books dealing with current happenings and ephemeral problems, many non-fiction works sell steadily for years, whereas the average first novel is dead within three months and often within three weeks after publication.

The fame which is popularly supposed to be attached to authorship, and the rank of superiority which is supposed to go with the appearance of one's name on the title page of a book, are, I think, even more responsible for the huge army of literary aspirants than is the desire for pecuniary gain. Especially is this the case with a considerable number of persons of both sexes who are either wealthy or socially important or both, and whose names grace the covers of so many books. It is this, too, more by far than the desire for profit, that is responsible for the publication every year, at their authors' expense, of so considerable a number of volumes of junk in prose and verse. It is this vanity, this desire for publication on the part of people of wealth and title, that is responsible, too, for the appearance in the daily and weekly Press of articles by men and women whose literary efforts have never gone beyond the signing of their names.

The notion that it is ridiculously easy to write is linked up with and largely the result of the coincident notion that authorship is the one profession where no training or apprenticeship is needed. At one time, the popular notion respecting authorship was that one could write or one couldn't write. Writing was looked upon as a gift from the gods, and to those so gifted the task was supposed to be simplicity itself. The average man or woman looked upon an author as a singularly gifted individual, worthy of a degree of respect which was mixed with a good deal of awe. It was, too, this widely practised genuflection on the part of the ordinary person to the members of the profession of letters that, naturally and inevitably, caused the author metaphorically to cock his hat on one side and think himself no end of an important fellow. Today the pendulum has swung to the other extreme with a vengeance. Thanks to the tremendous extension of free educational facilities; to the vastly enhanced self-assurance among adolescents of both sexes; to the growing editorial policy of publishing articles over the signatures of unintelligent and often illiterate social, sporting and stage celebrities; to the extensive advertising by the schools of journalism to the effect that every individual blessed with the ability to write a letter can be turned into a successful writer: thanks to all these factors functioning coincidentally, the average man and woman, schoolboy and schoolgirl, are all convinced that they are capable of writing for the Press. Typists, shop assistants, clerks, business men, in fact all who have been granted that doubtful blessing known as a secondary-school education, criticise current literature with assurance and industry, they all irradiate confidence in their ability to write something themselves that will be just as good as and probably a good deal better than anything they have read. To a very big extent it is owing to this widespread belief, that the post-office vans are cluttered with manuscripts that have not the faintest prospect of ever gracing the printed page; that publishers' readers and editors lament the piles of literary junk that litter their desks. It is to this self-same belief that so many thousands of people are continually asking themselves the question (and incidentally usually answering it in the affirmative) with which I commenced this chapter.

Now if by becoming a writer is meant emulating the work of James Joyce, or climbing to the heights of fame reached by George Bernard Shaw, or producing 'best-sellers' with the ease and sureness of J.B. Priestley; then I fear the answer, so far as are concerned 9,999 out of every 10,000 of these aspirants, is decidedly no. But if, to the contrary, is meant is it *possible* for one who is prepared to go through a certain specific, long and arduous apprenticeship to make money out of writing, the answer is a very different one. In a proportion – a considerable proportion – of such cases it is possible to get into print in some form or other; in a lesser proportion of such cases it is possible to supplement one's income; and in a minority of such cases it is possible to earn a living by writing.

There are, of course, certain essential fundamental qualifications. These basic qualifications are, in these days of universal education, possessed by the majority. And, in most cases where they are not actually present, they can be mastered. The essentials are: (1) the ability to read accurately; (2) the ability to write simple sentences free from the more obvious grammatical errors.

It is a queer thing that, alone among the professions, journalism should be considered to require no training. There is, for instance, nobody holding the view that one could become a competent and successful doctor, or a lawyer, or even a parson, without going through a long and expensive apprenticeship. But the fiction that no such apprenticeship is essential in the case of authorship persists and flourishes year in and year out. It *is* a fiction. And sooner or later every literary aspirant discovers for himself that it is a fiction. He finds that an apprenticeship, and a long apprenticeship at that, is *essential*. Moreover, he finds that, unlike most professions, *the fact of serving this apprenticeship does not in itself ensure success*. It is not a mere matter of passing an examination, or of being articled for a period of years, and then automatically entering the chosen profession; to the contrary, it is a matter of mastering the technique of writing articles and books that are of saleable quality; and, having written them, of mastering another difficult art, that of selling them. It is because of these difficulties that each year thousands of aspirants, after months or years of effort, disillusioned and disappointed, give up the game in despair and disgust.

The journalist, and especially the unknown journalist, has his expenses too. That, largely because of their nature, they are overlooked by the inexperienced and rarely mentioned in textbooks for writers, does not alter the fact of their existence. In instance, the postage account alone is a considerable item; then there are the various matters of envelopes, reference books, magazines and newspapers. And paper. In the writing of a full-length (70,000 words) non-fiction book, allowing for wastage and corrections, a minimum of 1500 sheets of paper is often used: 500 for the first draft, 500 for the typescript itself and a further 500 for the duplicate copy. In a year the total expenditure on these items represents a sum which will come as a surprise to any one who has dismissed it as a mere bagatelle.

We have now arrived at the point where it is admitted that, by any man or woman of mature intelligence, *the art of writing to the literary standard required by the average newspaper, or popular magazine, or trade journal, can be acquired*. It can be acquired by a careful study of the work of literary craftsmen, by a mastery of the essentials of composition, by much practice, by steady plodding industry, by great patience, and by an inexhaustible amount of perseverence. These factors are essential to success in the fields of ordinary free-lance journalism. Writing for the literary reviews, or the so-called highbrow magazines, is very decidedly another matter.

The old idea that the art of expressing oneself in words is a gift from the gods is so much bunkum. The companion idea that every successful author conveys his ideas to paper without conscious effort, the words flowing from the tip of his pen as if by magic, is also, to a very big extent, plain bunkum. There are, true enough, authors of a certain type who can write or dictate at considerable speed; but for every one of these there are a cool hundred who find the task a laborious one. There are authors with several fine works to their credit, who turn out their masterpieces slowly and with infinite labour. *Madame Bovary* was the work of years; Conrad laboured at his books with huge patience; so did Robert Louis Stevenson; James Joyce worked for seven years at *Ulysses* before he wrote finis to the manuscript; D.H. Lawrence re-wrote the script of *Lady Chatterley's Lover* three times before he was satisfied with it.

But whether the turning out of the manuscript be a protracted affair or a quick one; the actual acquirement of the technique of writing is inevitably a slow and difficult process.

How can this essential technique be acquired by the literary aspirant? There are three recognised ways. The first is for the youth who aspires to journalism to get into a newspaper office, either as an office boy or as a pupil, and in this way learn the art of writing for the Press from the ground up. This method, however, may, so far as this book is concerned, be ignored. It is, in the first place, a method necessarily restricted to the few, as there are obviously a limited number only of such openings available. It is, moreover, restricted in its application because the majority of writers never discover the itch for authorship until it is too late to become either an office boy or a pupil. More import, however, is the fact that work in a newspaper office, excellent though it may be as a training ground for a reporter or a member of the editorial staff, is of dubious value as training for a writer of books.

The method *usually* adopted is to bombard the editorial offices and the publishers with manuscripts of every length and description, until either through sheer dismay one gives up in despair, or a number of acceptances leads one to continue the bombardment until a regular income is secured. What, in point of fact, the beginner really does in this case is to teach himself the technique of authorship through actual experience.

There is a third way and an increasingly popular one – to become a pupil at one of the schools of journalism. It is hotly and recurrently debated whether the beginner would be better advised to keep his money in his pocket. The answer to the problem depends upon two things: (1) the pupil himself, (2) the nature of the school. If the beginner is not prepared to read widely and to study diligently, to labour indefatigably at the task of writing, to profit by his errors; in short, to put his whole heart and soul into the task of mastering the art, no tuition will be of the faintest use to him. But if he is prepared to do all this, then the correspondence course, *provided it is a good one*, may be of some help; it will probably shorten his term of apprenticeship by enabling him to avoid many errors and preventing him wasting his time in unprofitable directions.

I say *if* the correspondence course is a good one. *The proviso is of supreme importance.* Fees paid to a dud school of journalism represent not only money thrown down the gutter, but may easily *extend* the term of apprenticeship instead of shortening it. Before paying any fees it is well to make some inquiries as to the literary capabilities of the professor, teacher, literary expert, or whatever precise title the actual corrector of manuscripts goes by. If he is not a writer himself with published works to his credit, it may safely be assumed that he has tried and failed, and obviously therefore his advice and corrections are of the smallest value. But the correspondence course is not essential. It does not matter which precise method one adopts so long as one slogs at it long enough and energetically enough to master the essential technique.

Now although the art of confecting English good enough for the requirements of the average newspaper or popular periodical can be acquired in one of the ways I have mentioned, the mere acquirement of this art is not, in itself, sufficient to ensure success as a writer. It is not enough to enable one to dredge from that most precarious of all professions – free-lance journalism – a *living wage*. Something more than the mere mastery of sentence construction is required – were this not so, every professor of English at the colleges throughout the country would be an author of repute. But what is the truth? These professors and teachers are bombarding the editorial and publishing offices with as little average success as are the hosts of literary aspirants gracing other walks in life. The reason for this calls for no diligent search. Grammatically perfect English can be and often is the most boring prose imaginable. The published works – usually at their authors' expense – of so many of these college professors prove this statement to the hilt. They express nothing but a string of platitudes couched in the most emasculated prose that ever gets between book covers.

The successful writer must have something to say, and he must say it in a way that is refreshing, interesting, provoking or amusing. It is because of the necessity of these additional points that success in the world of literature is so difficult to achieve. For while the mere technique of sentence construction is acquirable by the average educated individual, the additional and vitally important knack of injecting this necessary life-blood is not acquirable by everyone. It calls for intelligence as opposed to mere education: for wide acquaintance with life as opposed to mere book knowledge.

Thus success depends neither upon what is referred to as an aptitude for writing, nor upon an expensive education. These factors may be useful, but largely they are adventitious. The one who writes easily and voluminously may never confect a line worth reading. The one who sweats and struggles for a solid hour over a dozen lines may turn out something of great merit and importance. It may be grammatically bad, the spelling may be atrocious, but if it contains an idea worth preserving in print, there is hope for that writer. The technique of writing can be acquired. What cannot be acquired, in the huge majority of cases, is intelligent thinking, or the basic idea for an article or a book.

2

THE GENERAL TECHNIQUE
OF WRITING

AIMING AT CLARITY

I have mentioned how essential it is that the beginner should master the art of sentence construction. It is equally necessary for him to cultivate a clear, crisp, lively style of writing. Also while it is well not to be hide-bound by the canons of grammar, certain rules must be observed.

It cannot be too often repeated or too strongly stressed that, in itself, grammatical accuracy does not make a manuscript acceptable. Something more than this is required. Nor, conversely, do the presence of errors in technique necessarily lead to the rejection of a manuscript or to its failure when published. There are scores of successful books and hundreds of articles published every year which bristle with grammatical blunders. But these are successes in spite of their technical faults and not because of them: a point it is well that the slovenly and ignorant should never for a moment overlook.

The main aim of every writer should be to present his work, whether it be an article or a book, in sentences which unfold his meaning with the clarity of crystal. Invariably should the writer ask himself this important question: Is my meaning perfectly clear to the reader?

To this one outstanding rule is every other rule of writing subservient. Beauty of phrase, novelty of wording; admirable though they be, are of little value if the meaning of the sentence is blurred or ambiguous; or if the thesis presented is marred by tiresome repetition, confusion of thought, or patently illogical conclusions.

Second only to this is the need to present the matter in an original manner. Dullness in writing is an unforgivable sin. It leads to the rejection of at least seventy-five per cent of the manuscripts submitted every day to editors and publishers. Interest is largely dependent upon style in writing, but also to some extent is it dependent upon the choice of words.

Actually it all boils down to the use of the right word in the right place. The competent writer is rarely faced with any doubt as to which particular word out of a number of alternatives to use in order to express in the clearest and most adequate manner possible that which he wishes to convey.

The error which every beginner makes is one of superfluity. He uses too many sentences to get his ideas upon paper, and too many words in each sentence. Most writers, even successful writers, to some extent fail to observe this golden rule of economy in words. Partly is this due to the general notion that a mass of words conceals poverty of thought. It does no such thing. It merely emphasises it.

Every unnecessary word tends to weaken a sentence, just as every unnecessary sentence tends to weaken an article or a book. This does not necessarily mean that a short sentence is always better than a long one, as is often urged in textbooks on composition. A short sentence may contain superfluous words; while from a long sentence it may be impossible to cut out a single word without weakening the force or altering the meaning of that sentence. Where the short sentence has the advantage over the long one is in its applicability to the needs of the beginner. It is easier, for one unversed in the intricacies of writing, to express oneself clearly by the use of short sentences. But a practised author will experience no such difficulty.

It is advisable, though not essential, that the writer should have a working acquaintance with the rules of grammar. I don't mean by this that he should necessarily observe these rules on every occasion. But it should always be remembered that the one who is in the best position to break a grammatical rule is the one who is thoroughly acquainted with that rule. It is one thing to violate a principle of sentence construction knowingly and for greater effect, it is quite another to blunder into the breach unwittingly and thus perpetrate an ugly and a clumsy sentence.

In instance, there is the age-old problem of the split infinitive. So much has been made of this in textbooks on composition compiled by those dullest of all writers, professors of English, that the beginner feels that to allow a split infinitive to appear in his manuscript will damn its chances of acceptance at once. And as a result he makes tortured efforts to avoid any such *faux pas*. Most practised writers, too, avoid the split infinitive, not so much because of any real objection to it but through the fear of being accused of ignorance of grammatical rules. The writer who wishes to get the best and clearest effects will not hesitate to split an infinitive, when he thinks the force and clarity of the sentence will thereby be improved. And undeniably there are such occasions. To present one example, 'failure to completely comprehend' is a better and less ambiguous constructional form than 'failure completely to comprehend.'

The best rule to adopt in every case where an improvement will be effected by splitting an infinitive is to do so without any hesitation, but in all other cases to follow the orthodox rule. And this is the line of reasoning that should be adopted in regard to all *sound* grammatical rules.

On the other hand many grammatical rules are merely silly. Thus the rule that no sentence should commence with 'And' or 'But,' and the equally absurd admonition that the last word in a sentence should never be a preposition. If the force of a sentence can be emphasised by the use of a final vigorous preposition, there need be no hesitation in its use.

AVOIDING THE DEADLIEST OF SINS

Much nonsense has been written about style. It is a result of this nonsense that the idea is current among amateur writers that style necessarily means elegant diction, high-faluting terminology, and original sentence construction. Evolve a style of your own is the advice given in so many of the handbooks on journalism.

It is through reading essays on the importance of culti-vating an individual style that the aspiring free-lance who aims to get his stuff into the popular magazines and Sunday news-sheets, apes the mannerisms of the modernistic littérateurs, and produces copy that he has no more chance of ever seeing in print between the covers of a popular periodical or gracing the columns of the Sunday Press than he has of witnessing a snowstorm in the Sahara desert.

Style is more important than matter, says one literary tutor; pay great attention to the development of an individ-ual style says another; style is everything in writing says a third. Nearly every teacher of English quotes Buffon's aphorism 'the style is the man.' The lot of them ignore or overlook Swift's succinct and revealing statement: 'Style may be defined, proper words in proper places.'

Style, so far as it means either fine writing or bizarre writing, is no concern of the free-lance with a living to earn. The only style that he requires is a clear, concise, crisp form of expression, free from all superfluities, redundancies, clichés and old-fashioned journalese. Neither the neologisms nor mannerisms of the neo-sophisticated school, on the other hand; nor the ponderous, dreary, platitudinous English of the college professor, on the other, is wanted.

Readers of newspaper articles want the news or the facts; they care nothing for niceties in the writing.

This does not mean that individualism in writing is to be discouraged; it does not mean that slovenliness is advisable; it does not mean that the rules of syntax are to be grossly violated. What it does mean is that the beginner must not get it into his head that in the cultivation of fine writing lies the secret of success, that perfection in the art of stringing together beautiful phrases will make up for lack of knowledge con-cerning the subject of his article or for weakness in the plot of his story. It will do neither the one thing nor the other.

What we are concerned with is the production of saleable articles and books rather than in the pursuit of *le mot juste*. I am not going to say that it is not possible to produce a 'best-seller' by employing the methods of a Flaubert. There are instances by the dozen where writers of unquestioned literary ability have earned most satisfactory incomes. Arnold Bennett did, Anatole France did, Thomas Hardy did, Mark Twain did, Thackeray did, Dickens did, George Moore did, John Galsworthy did. But at the same time there are, in this country and in America, writers by the score, of exceptional ability, whose earnings are not those of a bank clerk. There are others who, deprived of alien methods of earning their livings, or of their private incomes, and dependent solely on the profits from their books, would quickly starve.

Granted that one has something to say which the public wants to hear, the manner of saying it may be poor, good or brilliant. It depends largely upon the manner of saying it whether or not it will ever see print.

Clearly written English is good English; muddled English is bad English. Observe that I am referring to the writing, and not to the thoughts expressed in that writing. The idea that clear writing and exact reasoning are necessarily synonymous is a popular myth. It is a myth broadcasted by school teachers, lecturers on English, *et all*. If you want evidence of this statement being a myth you need not search either far or diligently. Who in all the world ever wrote clearer English than Shaw, and who, in his biological divagations, ever perpetrated a more thorough example of muddled thinking. And there is Chesterton, there is Belloc, there is Wells. On the other hand some of the most incisive thinkers that have ever lived have written atrociously; their arguments have been most difficult to follow owing to the muddled manner in which they have been put on paper. Spinoza was one such. Kant was another. Theodore Dreiser has made every literary blunder possible and yet stands out as a master of clear thinking.

Thus we reach some definite idea as to what constitutes perfection in style. In an article or in a non-fiction book (and these exhaust what we are concerned with in this work) the argument must be lucidly given, the manner of presentation must be bright and interesting, the whole thesis must be concisely stated. These are the essentials. Precisely what steps the individual writer may take to attain a style which conforms to this definition matters little. In the process he may observe or he may break rules of grammar; he may use neologisms; he may copy other writers; he may even change his method of writing in the course of the book. In this, at any rate, the end *does* justify the means.

For logical presentation of thought few can hope to equal Swift. The style adopted by Swift possessed all the attributes I have just elaborated, and was the best style for his particular purpose Swift could possibly have chosen. Similarly, T.H. Huxley, for sheer clarity of writing, had no peer. Frank Harris was another writer remarkable for his clarity. George Bernard Shaw, James Branch Cabell, Wyndham Lewis, Aldous Huxley, jump to my mind.

Nothing militates against this logical presentation of thought so much as a profusion of words. And seeing that wordiness is a fault with ninety-nine per cent of literary amateurs and fifty per cent of professional writers, some idea will be gained of the number whose style is afflicted with this particular distemper. Artsibashev realised this when he gave examples of the two literary styles in use among Russian novelists. One stylist would say: 'I will shoot you like a dog!' The other would amplify this bald statement into: 'I am thinking of shooting you. How shall I shoot you? All my life I have been very fond of dogs, but if a dog offended me, I would shoot it down without mercy. I am not certain I shall not do the same by you.' There may be some slight exaggeration here, but Artsibashev's examples should be kept big in mind by every writer. They convey an invaluable lesson in the art of writing.

Sheer excellence of style can rarely make up for lack of something to say. It can, in its originality, its interest, or its humour, make up for lack of newness. The same old subject matter can be presented in a new way. Here it is precisely that style comes into its own: the ability to present the old facts or arguments in a new and attractive way will do much towards securing acceptance and publication.

Having arrived at a definition of style, how is the young writer to proceed in order to acquire a manner of writing that embodies these essentials; i.e., lucidity, brightness, conciseness. The first essential is largely a matter of syntax; a mastery of the principles of grammatical composition will do much to ensure the acquisition of a lucid manner of writing.

The other attributes of style – brightness and conciseness – can best be acquired by *closely studying other writers, and by imitation*. The advice so repeatedly given in textbooks to study but never imitate, is bosh. What is the good of studying the methods of other writers if one doesn't imitate them? The late Edgar Wallace's advice should be noted by every beginner: 'Don't be afraid of being a copy-cat. Imitate shamelessly, but choose the right master.' Actually every writer the world has known has imitated some predecessor or contemporary. Shakespeare copied unblushingly; Stevenson, in his continuous imitation, came perilously near actual plagiarism. But there is an art in imitation. It lies, this art, not so much in taking one individual writer and slavishly copying his method, as Stevenson did; as in studying a number of selected writers, and by adopting certain methods and mannerisms of each and blending them into a new conglomeration, acquiring a style which, while it owes everything to imitation, has some trait of distinction, insomuch as it is not precisely a duplication of any *one* in particular. This has been the method adopted, consciously or unconsciously, by all authors since the appearance of the first book.

There is one book that every literary aspirant should study, and he should study it with the closest attention. That book is the Bible. It is the style book *par excellence*.

One must always keep an eye on the trend of fashion. There is fashion in technique as in everything else. This is one reason why it is so unprofitable to study the majority of the dead, and quite a number of living, writers. There are, however, those whose prose will always repay close study. There is Swift, there is Hazlitt, there is Matthew Arnold, there is Pater, there is James Huneker, there is Frank Harris, there is George Moore, there is T.H. Huxley. There is Shaw, Cabell, Aldous Huxley, David Garnett, Richard Aldington.

Not all great writers are to be copied. There is danger, grave danger, in attempting to copy the inimitable. For instance, any attempt to imitate James Joyce is inadvisable. Many have tried and have come to grief.

A CATALOGUE OF DO'S AND DON'TS

Nothing in all the world damns a manuscript so much as a peppering with clichés; nothing in all the world is so sure to stamp it as the work of a beginner, or one who has failed to master the technique of the writer. For, apart from amateurs the only professional journalists who employ, with any degree of profusion, rubber-stamped phrases, are editors of and contributors to provincial news-sheets, trade papers, poultry and rabbit journals, church magazines, sports supplements, *et all*.

It should, however, be remembered that a cliché becomes a cliché through constant repetition. Writers are accused of using clichés when what they have actually done is to invent them. The neologism of to-day becomes the cliché of to-morrow. Thus a list of rubber-stamped phrases is complete – in the fullest possible sense of the word – only on the day it is compiled. The efficient writer uses a new word or phrase, whether it is coined or lifted from another source, just so long as it is *new* – the moment it is in danger of becoming a cliché he ceases to use it.

The list which follows is a comprehensive one. It is not implied that these phrases should *never* be used, for obviously there are circumstances where many of them can be advantageously employed. But every writer should use them *sparingly* and only when no alternative terminology is available.

abject terror
acid test
advanced threateningly
adorably sweet
amazingly handsome
at the parting of the ways
attractive girl
awfully nice
awfully sweet
bathed in tears
be this as it may
better half
bitter sneer
blind alley
blue funk
boiling over with indignation
bone of contention
bounding upstairs
brilliant novelist

bullying tone
bursting with rage
but it was not to be
captured the imagination
cement our relations
challenging smile
chattering teeth
come to stay
common or garden
conscience stricken
conspicuous by its absence
consummation devoutly to be wished
cordially endorsed his remarks
cosy room
cowers weakly
crash of thunder
crass ignorance
cringing movement
crying shame
cup that cheers but does not inebriate
curate's egg
curses not loud but deep
daring aviator
daring robbery
dash for freedom
dead cert
defiant sneers
defied analysis
definitely superior
denizens of the deep
desirable residence
determined suicide
devouring element
did not deny the soft impeachment
disciple of Bacchus
distinguished diplomat
eagle eye
elude their vigilance
eminent counsel
exception proves the rule, the

exclusive club
exclusive gathering
eyeing him keenly
fascinating pursuit
famous actress
feast of reason, the
few equals and no superior
fidgeting uneasily
fierce jealousy
fierce sarcasm
filled with horror
filthy lucre
flew into a rage
food for thought
forlorn hope
fragrant weed
fusilade of bullets
gentle art of Izaak Walton
gentlemen of the Press
glaring with hate
green-eyed monster, the
grim tragedy
growing rage
guilty terror
has the defects of its qualities
heir of all the ages
horrified eyes
howling wilderness
hurrying breathlessly
immaculate clothes
in a hard metallic voice
in a tone of mingled rage and relief
in durance vile
in exasperation
inner man
intrepid aviator
intrepid explorer
intriguing book
in well-informed political circles
irony of fate, the

it is alleged
jerking himself up
jumping nervously to his feet
last but not least
laughing scornfully
leave severely alone
let it severely alone
life was found to be extinct
logic of events, the
long arm of coincidence, the
made the supreme sacrifice
meaning grin, a
metal more attractive
mocking laugh
mocking voice
missing link.
more in sorrow than in anger
more sinned against than sinning
must be seen to be believed
muttering with rage
neat dress
needless to relate
no mean adversary
not wisely but too well
of inestimable value
olive branch
on the knees of the gods
one's quiver full
outer man
parting of the ways, the
paralysed with terror
plods his weary way
prophetic evil
psychological moment
quivering body
rain came down in torrents
rash act
received a *coup de grace*
sacred edifice
sensational escape

21

seriously inclined
scantily clad
scenes he loved so well
scour the neighbourhood
she discoursed sweet music
she went deathly cold
sickening thud
silence that said volumes
simply furious
sleep the sleep of the just
smiled mockingly
snort of contempt
sniff of contempt
socially prominent
sorry plight
speed demon
split second
spread like wildfire
squealing with terror
staggering to his feet
staring moodily
strange charm
strikes a responsive chord in their hearts
stunning blow
succulent bivalve
such for instance
sudden confusion
sudden fear
sweetly pretty
take in each other's washing
taunting laugh
tender mercies
terrible discovery
terrifically good
tears of mortification
there's the rub
thinking gloomily
this auspicious occasion
threatening glare
threatening step

thumping lie
tiny flat
to be or not to be
too funny for words
tragic sigh
training the young idea how to shoot
trembling fingers
turning angrily
turning her back on him with contempt
unconsidered trifles
veritable *multum in parvo*, a
vicious circle
vivid flash of lightning
waning strength
was the recipient of
waiting nervously
weeping hysterically
wild laugh
winced as if she had been struck
wave of passion
we venture to conclude
with a little cry of pain
with a shudder of horror
with a start of surprise
with a forced laugh
with a grim smile
with a grunt
with a groan of despair
with a malicious grin
with a scornful smile
with a snort of rage
with a start
with bravado
young hopeful
young and pretty
your letter was greatly appreciated

Write
    abound *in*
    accord *with*

adequate *to*, not adequate for
averse *to*
alien *to*
aim *at*, not aim to
all right, not alright
amid not amidst
among, not amongst
acquiesced *in*, not acquiesced to
as well as, not equally with
behind, not at the back of
better than, not superior to
burned, not burnt
capacity *for*
carcass, not carcase
clothes, not attire
compare *with*, not compare to
comes from, not hails from
connected with, not identified with
conversant *with*
culminated *in*, not culminated by
derogatory *to*, not derogatory from
died, not passed away
differ *from*
different *from*, not different to or different than
if, not provided that
I intend *to do*, not I intend doing
I *should* like, not I would like
immune *from*, not immune to
in a ship, not on a ship
in order to, not with a view to
in the event *that*, not in the event of
inculcate *in*, not inculcate with
indifferent *to*
infuse *into*, not infuse with
inquire, not enquire
instil *into* not instil with
lend, not loan
made a speech, not delivered a speech
make an experiment, not try an experiment
married, not wed

mentioned, not alluded to
named, not by the name of
need *of*
oblivious *of*, not oblivious to
on to, not onto
other than, not different than
parallel *with*
perpendicular *to*
preference *to*, not preference over
preventive, not preventative
PS., not P.S.
pursuant *to*
substitute *for*, not substitute by
that is not *so*, not that is not the case
that kind, not those kind
three times a week, not tri-weekly
try *to*, not try and
versed *in*
weight, not avordupois
whether or *not*, not whether or no
while, not whilst
with a view *to*
woman, not lady
write *to* you, not write you

Don't write
a *mutual* friend
advance *on*
all of
almost quite – omit one or the other
an historical, *an* habitual, *an* hotel, *an* hypothesis – always
    use *a*
apparent error
approve *of*
as to whether
authoress
both alike
but what
canine species for dog
compensated *for*

connect *up*
continue *on*
entirely extinct
equally *as well*
every now and then
funeral obsequies
got married
I am afraid there is going to be trouble, but I fear there
    is ...
if and when
in any shape or form
inside *of*
in the neighbourhood of, for about
kind of *a*
later *on*
male man – omit one or the other
more preferable
new beginner
no end of
on the street
outside *of*
pair of twins
perfectly straight
poetess
prior to
prox.
quite dead
refer back
remember *to*
repudiate, for deny
rodent, for rat
repeat *again*
save and except
say, for voice
seldom ever
self-confessed
small particle
still continued
think to
to have refused, for to refuse

26

two twins
ult.
very inexpensive
widow *woman*

remember that
agenda is plural
anybody and *anyone* are singular and should be followed
by *his* or *her*
amenable is always followed by *to*
cognizant is always followed by *of*
connive is followed by *at*
consequent is followed by *upon*
criterion is singular
data is plural; so is *strata*; so is *phenomena*
employee is both masculine and feminine
impervious is always followed by *to*
inimical is always followed by *to*
on should be used after *obligatory*
per cent requires no point
textbook should be written without a hyphen
United States of America is singular

Don't
overwork the article *the* – or the word *very*
make yourself ridiculous by striving to avoid using the
same word twice or thrice in a paragraph or on a page.
use an adjective with *unique*
use capitals for *angel, saint, city council*
use *evince* as a verb

Use
italics sparingly. They should be restricted to words or
phrases which it is essential should be emphasised.
Their promiscuous use defeats the writer's object.

Avoid
or use sparingly words that have been worked to death,
e.g., *absolutely, camouflage, definitely, intrigued, prac-
tically, proposition.*

27

Use

capitals for: *Houses of Parliament, God, Virgin Mary, Saviour, Holy Ghost, Satan,* and pronouns referring to God – *His, He, Him.*

3

FINDING A TARGET

ARTICLE OR BOOK?

It is often said that the very fact of a young writer's name appearing on the title-page of a book constitutes an open sesame to literary success – that by virtue of this one fact itself he will find it much easier to secure acceptances for his work by magazine and newspaper editors; that, more and further, he is almost sure to find these self-same editors clamouring for the products of his pen.

During the course of my career as a literary free-lance, I can solemnly avow that as a *direct result* of the publication of my books, and over a period of some thirty years, I have had exactly seven articles, one short story and three pamphlets commissioned by English and American editors or publishers. Now before anyone hastens cynically to comment that these particular tomes decorated with my name have probably been all of the type that may be best described as unsaleable and unpopular, or, in other words, rank failures, let me say that one book has run into no fewer than fifteen editions; another into eight editions; a third into six editions; a fourth into five editions; and many others into two, three and four editions each.

Now for the other side of the story. The first two books I ever wrote were *both* commissioned by their respective publishers. I was writing articles at the time, and it was through the publication of these articles that the books were commissioned. My first book, the original edition of which was published as far back as 1910, went into four editions, and the odds are that if it had not been for this book being commissioned I should not, at that time at any rate, have given any attention to book-writing at all. Since those early days I have written twelve full-length books and three pamphlets all *commissioned* by their respective publishers.

It is true that I have written a very considerable number of commissioned articles, but what I wish to make clear is that these articles were commissioned by editors who had previously published contributions from my pen, and *these commissions had no connection whatever with my published books*.

Boiled down, my experience is that while the publication of articles may and probably will help in the task of getting books accepted or commissioned (in no sense an easy matter); the fact of having achieved the authorship of a book is, in itself, of precious little value in securing publication for an article.

Observe that I am not referring to authors of those phenomenal successes which occasionally dazzle the literary firmament. Nor am I referring to those monstrously lucky individuals who produce first novels which take the world by storm. What I am referring to are the authors of books, fiction and non-fiction, which achieve the ordinary run of popularity, with sales running anywhere between one thousand and five thousand copies – in other words, to ninety-nine per cent of all the authors who are engaged in the task of confecting books.

Because of all this *I advise the beginner to try his hand at writing articles before attempting the production of a book*.

There are rare and startling exceptions, true enough. But I am not concerned with exceptions. I am attempting to give advice, not to the genius, or to the lucky amateur, or to the beginner with influence, who does not require any advice at all; but to the ordinary ambitious novice at the writing game.

There are additional reasons why the beginner should attempt short pieces, at any rate at first. For one thing it is easier to write a number of short articles than it is to write a full-length book. For another thing, one has a lot more chances of striking oil – one can probably write at least thirty articles in the time that goes to the preparation of a book, and in consequence there are thirty chances to one chance of landing something. And finally, in nine cases out of ten the financial reward securable from a number of articles is very much more satisfactory than from the royalties earned by a book–and quicker.

PART II

ARTICLE WRITING AND GENERAL JOURNALISM

4

THE NEWSPAPER ARTICLE

THE QUESTION OF SCOPE

The market for newspaper articles varies considerably from time to time, in accordance with changes in editorial policy. A paper which, at one period, may use a considerable number of articles by outside contributors, may suddenly change the make-up and tone of its editorial page, and feature work produced by its own salaried staff only.

In recent years there has been a tendency to feature more and more what is known as the 'celebrity' article. One of the results of this policy is that in many of the leading daily and Sunday papers the free-lance has the smallest chance of getting an article into print. Those articles which are signed almost invariably bear the names of well-known actresses, film-stars, clerics, criminals, boxers, titled ladies and society beauties. Now it may be contended that in the end, seeing that these celebrities rarely do the actual writing themselves, it works out all right. For, as regards ninety-nine per cent of these articles, what really happens is this. A professional woman journalist writes an article on, say, 'Happiness as a Career,' and gets a popular actress to sign it; or she writes a column on 'Dress Sense' over the signature of Lady Bentfoot. In the one case an arrangement is made with the actress, and in the other with Lady Bentfoot, as to the division of the payment received for the article. Without these famous names the journalist could not sell her articles, as obviously dress sense by an unknown Sarah Jones is of no interest to the readers of the *Sunday Bulletin*; nor are the public clamouring to read Sarah's views on 'Happiness as a Career.' So the journalist earns her money, and it may be argued that it does not matter anyway: that the actress and the titled lady are really helping the journalist to make money and not depriving her of a job. This is true as far as it goes, but unfortunately it does not go very far. Sarah Jones is doing nothing to build up a journalistic reputation – she is dependent upon finding a continuous supply of celebrities for whom she can 'ghost' – that is, if she is an unattached writer. But, often enough, Sarah Jones is not a free-lance at all; usually she is on the editorial staff of the paper which prints the article. It is customary, particularly in cases of autobiographies, reminiscences, and fashion columns, for the editor to arrange to pay the celebrities for the use of their names and give the job of writing the articles to a member of his staff. More often than not therefore it is staff work, and the free-lance has a poor chance of breaking in.

This editorial policy of printing articles over the signatures of celebrities has, too, a significance which the young writer should not overlook. It means that the opinions or views of writers who have not achieved some degree of fame or notoriety, either in literary circles or elsewhere, are not wanted. The soundness of the views expressed, the excellence of the writing, are minor points. An atrociously written article over the signature of the Countess of Timbuctoo, displaying opinions that would discredit a twelve-year-old schoolgirl, is infinitely preferable, from an editor's point of view, to an article on the same subject by one possessed of expert knowledge and a style reminiscent of Pater.

Increasingly, therefore, does the free-lance find himself compelled to turn to the popular weeklies, to the provincial Press, and to the trade and technical papers. The popular weeklies provide exceedingly good markets. They pay well for the stuff they print. They are ready buyers of bright, interesting, informative articles. Naturally, however, with so huge a number of writers turning out manuscripts of every conceivable brand, these popular journals are subjected to what is little less than a bombardment, and competition is razor-edged in its keenness. All things considered, therefore, the provincial Press presents perhaps the most favourable field for the beginner, and even here, his task is no easy one. Probably every provincial newspaper receives each week much more printable matter from outside sources than it can possibly use. True, the number of provincial papers, daily and weekly, is a considerable one; but despite their number, actual requirements in the way of matter from outside contributors are relatively small. Apart from the local news items, the bulk of the magazine-page contents in nearly all provincial newspapers is syndicated stuff. There are a few short articles required for the leader page and that is about all.

Here, indeed, we touch upon the trouble which applies to writing for all the newspapers, both London and provincial, and all the popular weeklies as well – the market is badly overcrowded. The difficulty which the free-lance journalist of any competence experiences is not in the production of copy sufficiently good to satisfy editorial requirements, but in *selling his articles when they are written*. For it is a relatively safe assumption that every paper of the types mentioned receives five times more matter of printable standard than it can use. This fact, and fact it is, rarely receives mention in books for the guidance of the literary aspirant; more rarely still does it receive mention in any advertisement or prospectus emanating from a school of journalism. The young writer is often heard to remark that the stuff that is printed in a certain periodical is not one whit better than his own work which this very paper has rejected. Often this is true. It is true because of the very point I have mentioned above. And for this very reason it is essential that the beginner, unless he wishes to trust entirely to that will-o'-the-wisp called luck, should turn out articles of exceptional interest. In this way, and in this way only, can he ensure acceptance.

In ninety-nine cases out of a hundred the beginner writes about subjects which, *from his pen*, have not the ghost of a chance of being accepted by any editor in the whole wide world. Basing his methods on the published articles by famous authors, politicians and celebrities, he writes essays displaying his opinions on various social and political problems. He is wasting time and money. Editors don't want the opinions of unknown writers – *not on any single subject under the sun*. Or he bombards every newspaper listed in *The Writers' and Artists' Year Book* with articles relating to subjects which happen to be in the news at the moment. Here again, in the huge majority of instances, all this work represents sheer waste of effort. For, by the time the free-lance's article reaches the editor, the topic with which it deals is probably, from the editor's viewpoint, as dead as King Solomon. Topical articles, in the overwhelming main, are either written on the spot by one of the staff, or they are urgently commissioned by the editor.

Probably fifty per cent of the articles submitted to every editor in London are dry-as-dust essays that might have come from the pen of a college professor. Dull as a textbook on economics; they are filled with empty rhetoric, their writers have nothing to say.

The two golden rules for all writers are: (1) Have something to say; (2) Stop writing the moment you have said it.

To this end avoid the superfluous word, the superfluous sentence, the superfluous paragraph.

In writing for the popular press, avoid anything that smacks of what is termed 'highbrow' literature. Avoid fine phraseology and unusual terminology. The popular Press does not give a hoot for literary merit. Its readers would not and could not recognise any such thing.

'Highbrow' literature is rarely profitable. It may, or may not, be more difficult to write than what is commonly termed journalistic tripe – the point is debatable. But what is certainly not debatable is that, with rare exceptions, the novelists and journalists who are knocking out steady and satisfactory livings from writing are producing little that is of actual *literary* merit.

It is all very well to sneer at the brewer of popular fiction and Sunday-newspaper articles, but one should not overlook the fact that this type of writer may, at any rate in the present economic dispensation, *prefer* to turn out well-paid journalistic junk rather than sweat over the confection of badly paid-literature. Possibly he has a living to earn, and experience has taught him that in the writing game it pays to turn out in quantities the stuff that is in demand by the editors of the popular papers. Producing work of high literary merit for microscopic payment, or possibly for no payment at all, possesses little appeal to the starving scribbler. Moreover, there is always the possibility of what, according to contemporary standards of criticism, ranks as journalist junk, becoming, in later ages, classical literature. It has happened so many times. Defoe's *Robinson Crusoe* was a piece of hack writing; of the same calibre were the bulk of Addison's essays; so, too, was much of Sir Walter Scott's work; and so, too, was Stevenson's *Treasure Island*. But the professors of English at the colleges and schools have, in their wisdom, selected the works of these authors for inclusion in that most dubious gallery known as 'the classics,' and those members of the public who like to pose as literary epicures have applauded these selections with resounding hosannas.

Perhaps the type of article mostly in demand today is the one best described as a 'News' article. The primary object of a newspaper is to give its readers news. In considering an article the editor asks himself: (1) Is the subject of this article news? and (2) Is it presented, or will it lend itself to presentation, in news form? Now the essence of news, from a newspaper standpoint, is exaggeration. This exaggeration may be explicit or it may be implicit; it may be suggested by over-emphasis of a feature or by the subduement or deletion of another feature, but exaggeration there must be just the same. There is no actual distortion in the facts themselves – the distortion is one of effect through the manner of presentation of those facts. This is the secret of the newspaper feature writer's craft. The nearer the free-lance can get to mastering this technique the greater will be his number of acceptances.

The 'story' must have human interest. This is another secret of the writer's craft. Look through the articles in your daily or weekly newspaper and observe how the human note is emphasised in nearly every one of them. More and more is this human touch required by the modern newspaper editor.

The beginner is forever being told that originality and success march hand in hand. The cry for originality is indeed an ever-recurring one. In the days of my nonage I took this cry seriously and, in consequence, I wasted much time and labour. Now I know better. I know, and every editor knows, and every writer of experience knows, that anything which smacks of originality in any *real* sense of the word is the last thing that is wanted in a popular newspaper article today. The only writer who can get an original idea or any form of advanced thought into the popular press is an author whose fame is so great that his opinions are 'news.'

37

The free-lance, therefore, who wishes to see his stuff in print, should never present any advanced, daring or novel viewpoint. In fact he should be chary of expressing any *opinion* at all.

The reason for this, if one reflects a minute, stares at one in all its barefaced truth. An editor has his readers to consider. These readers, in the huge main, possess rubber-stamped minds. They are morons. They skim the newspapers, they gape at the illustrated tabloids, they glue their eyes to the television. The result is they all think alike, they all see alike, they all have the same mental reactions and prejudices. Some of these prejudices are violent ones. And so far as are concerned ninety-nine per cent of the newspaper-reading public, if they pick up their matutinal gossip-sheet or hebdomadal garbage-bulletin and, after chuckling over the spicy police reports and gaping round-eyed at the advertisements of ladies' underwear, they find a column devoted to some writers' advanced ideas on sex, they are apt to rise up in hot indignation, hurl the shameless sheet into the fireplace, and cancel their order for that particular paper.

Do not be misled by the originality, outspokenness and daring manner in which tabooed and controversial subjects are discussed between book covers. Books and periodicals are entirely different propositions. Books do not cater for regular daily and weekly subscribers, they are not concerned with the views of advertisers. Newspapers and magazines, with a minority of exceptions, are mightily concerned with both.

Any reference to sex, any exposure of a public evil, any revolutionary treatment of a subject, will damn an article's chances of acceptance. The beginner, seeing the interest that sex arouses, as illustrated in the featuring of criminal and civil court cases, is naturally enough inclined to think that sex articles will find favour with editors. He is wrong. Sex is one of the main features of nearly every newspaper in London, and certainly of most Sunday newspapers, but not a *direct* feature. It is dealt with *in the news*. The sex side of a criminal trial, or of a divorce case, is emphasised by headlines and by cuts, because this is news. By adopting this policy the paper does not run anything like so great a risk of being accused of pandering to the tastes of licentious readers as it would if outspoken articles dealing with sex problems were featured. So, if you wish to succeed as a free-lance, keep those pet ideas of yours about subjects such as sex, and any iconoclastic notions concerning controversial matters such as religion, securely behind your teeth.

Much the same thing applies to the exposure of evils. Occasionally, an evil may be the subject of a stunt but, generally speaking, an article written by a free-lance exposing an evil, however true the facts, would stand no chance of acceptance. People don't wish to have ugly ulcers laid bare, or evils exposed; they prefer to shut their eyes and persuade themselves that everything is all right. The newspapers, by exposing graft and crooked dealings, especially in political, theological and commercial circles, make powerful enemies who never forget or forgive, while the majority of the huge army of readers have forgotten all about the affair in a week.

Nearly every paper, daily and weekly, has what is known as a 'Woman's Page.' Actually the whole paper has a feminine appeal, but this 'Woman's Page' is a special regular feature, comprising short articles and paragraphs on fashion, health, beauty culture, home hints, and social gossip of interest peculiarly to women. It may be taken for granted that the bulk of the matter that appears is either written in the office by one of the staff, or is regularly supplied by an outside contributor who specialises in this kind of stuff. The openings for occasional contributions are therefore much fewer than would appear at first sight, but most papers are prepared to buy occasional smartly written articles or paragraphs. They must be brief, snappy, and bright. About 500 words is the outside length.

Beginners are often told there is a fortune awaiting the humorous writer. Well, there may be a fortune awaiting another Jerome K. Jerome, or another P.G. Woodhouse, or another Miles Kington; but as regards ordinary humorous articles, the average free-lance would be well advised to concentrate on some other line. The market for humour is decidedly a limited market, and the bulk of the stuff that gets into print is staff work.

There is, however, a ready market for what, for want of a better term, I will call the semi-humorous 'news-article' or 'human story,' in contradistinction to the farcical sketches and nonsensical articles featured in the purely humorous weeklies of the *Punch* type. The writer who can treat a news item semi-humorously, or who can provide a human-interest story in a humorous vein is sure of a ready market for his work with most of the dailies.

There remain for mention the purely literary magazines and reviews. Although these periodicals are usually closed fields to the average free-lance, they do accept articles from outside contributors. But the standard is high, and the market is a very limited one. In consequence, the supply usually is very much greater than the demand. The *unknown* free-lance therefore has little hope of having his articles accepted for publication in preference to those submitted by known and often distinguished writers. Only an article of brilliance or of outstanding merit has a chance of getting into print.

The free-lance who aims at producing work of relatively high literary merit may, with advantage, concentrate on writing articles to the standard demanded by these literary magazines and reviews. If he can write well enough, and if he continues his bombardment long enough, he may eventually meet with some success.

But no one should ever make the error of looking upon these journals as providing ready-made alternative markets for the stuff which has been written for and has been rejected by the popular weeklies. This, strangely enough, is the viewpoint taken by a considerable number of beginners.

Should a writer ever allow his work to be published without payment? It is often argued that he should rigidly refuse to have anything to do with an editor who, or a periodical which, makes any such suggestion; and in support of this advice Dr. Johnson's opinion that 'No man but a blockhead ever wrote except for money,' is eternally quoted. It is one of those facile aphorisms which are not true. Admittedly, this book is concerned, and concerned only, with writing for money. But even so, the beginner may find that the time spent in the production of a number of articles which are printed over his own name without pecuniary reward is not altogether wasted. *Nothing that helps to bring an unknown writer's name before the public is wasted.* Even letters in the correspondence columns of the more important journals, if he can get them printed (contrary to popular opinion, this is not easy) will prove of some help to the beginner. George Bernard Shaw, from the very commencement of his literary career, realised the value of keeping his name before the public, and there can be no doubt that his policy of self-advertisement has had a good deal to do with his phenomenal success.

Rates of payment bear no relation whatever to literary merit. There are several literary journals printing matter of outstanding merit only, which do not pay for contributions. They don't pay because they can't pay. On the other hand, there are papers which pay exceptionally high rates for what, judged by any literary standard worth the name, is mere drivel.

Apart from the fact that the correspondence columns afford a good practising ground for the beginner, there are a few periodicals which pay for all letters printed, while some of the popular weeklies offer prizes for selected letters. Others again pay for letters on special subjects or in certain circumstances. Very many years ago I was commissioned to contribute to a certain weekly journal a number of provocative letters in various styles of writing for publication over a variety of signatures.

TECHNIQUE

The free-lance who, for one reason or another, desires to concentrate on article writing, must be prepared to hammer at a number of editorial doors, turning out nearly every kind of article from the 'gossip' paragraph to the 5,000 word heavyweight.

Brevity is the first essential. There must be no padding. *Deal with facts only*. The article which presents interesting facts in an interesting way is always welcomed by an editor. It need not be new. It can be, and it very often is, a re-write of facts published twenty or fifty years ago. But these facts must be surveyed from a fresh angle, and presented in a different and an essentially modern manner.

The brilliance of George Bernard Shaw is a brilliance of manner and not of matter. The originality of Shaw is an originality in treatment, and not in fact. There is nothing actually new in Shaw. He merely presents antiquated opinions and viewpoints in new and often outrageous dresses. What Shaw has done so brilliantly others have done and are doing less sensationally and dramatically. In point of fact, as regards popular journalism in all its aspects, there is nothing else to do. For if a writer does happen to depart from the well-worn track, he finds his efforts frowned upon by the occupants of editorial chairs.

Be sure of your facts. Because so much that is superficial finds its way into the papers, it does not follow that accuracy as regards basic facts is not essential. A slip will probably bring letters to the editor's desk from half-a-hundred smart alecks.

Let me at this point reiterate how necessary it is to avoid fine writing. It is not wanted. Keep the sentences short and crisp, and above all let them be of such a degree of simplicity that a child of twelve years can thoroughly grasp their meaning. *Modern newspapers are written for child mentality.* They have to be if they are to prove successful. They are written for morons whose highest intellectual effort is seen in the solving of a crossword puzzle or the playing of a game of bridge.

The question of length is of some importance. It is useless to send a 1,000 word article to a paper which does not use anything beyond 800 word articles. Nor is it of any use to enclose a covering letter intimating that the editor may cut down the article to suit his requirements. *If the article is capably written it cannot be cut down without spoiling it. If it can be cut down without ill effects it is a badly-written or a badly-constructed article.*

One of the secrets of success in free-lance journalism lies in the cultivation of a capacity for turning out quantities of saleable stuff at a rapid rate.

This was Edgar Wallace's secret of success. It is the secret of success of scores of journalists today.

Do not be misled by 'news' stories about dressing-gown-clad authors who work a couple of hours a day, or of literary notabilities who turn out one book a year, or of those who take up their pens only when inspiration comes. There are such writers, true enough, but they are either authors of 'best-sellers' who, through sheer luck, have achieved that degree of fame which enables them to earn fat incomes with a minimum amount of labour, or they are literary dilettanti possessed of comfortable incomes derived from sources other than their pens.

The average free-lance journalist, who sells fifty per cent of the stuff he writes at ordinary market rates, and who fails to sell the remaining fifty per cent of it at all, cannot afford to wait for inspiration.

A big output is essential. And a big output means *work*. Let there be no mistake about this – it means regular and continuous work.

It is best to keep proper hours, setting oneself a definite minimum output for each day. For instance, the production of a minimum 3,000 words a day, typed and revised ready for press. It is little enough.

The necessity for quantity of production as well as quality of the work produced leads us to the question of how much time should the young writer, when once he has embarked upon a literary career in dead earnest, spend on revision? It is a nice point. The advice usually given is to revise and revise and revise again and again. Admirable as is this advice during the period of apprenticeship which every writer must necessarily serve, when this period of apprenticeship is ended the matter is upon an entirely different footing.

Anatole France, we are told, wrote and re-wrote every paragraph in his manuscripts six times before he was satisfied. Well, this might have been a profitable course for the famous French novelist to adopt; and it may be all well and good for the wealthy dabbler in literature; but for the free-lance who has a living to earn and who has not had the luck to achieve fame, it is, in the majority of instances, an impracticable method. Were he to re-write each article two or three times, he would never be able to turn out sufficient copy to earn bread and butter. At the other extreme, slipshod writing will never get the beginner anywhere.

Much depends on the kind of stuff that is being written. For instance, a book or a novel calls for more care in its writing than does an ephemeral article or a short-story for one of the popular weeklies. It is safe to say that too much time cannot be spent on the revision of anything that is destined to appear between book covers. But where the markets aimed at are the popular magazines, the women's pages of the daily newspapers, the snappy weeklies, the trade journals; it is entirely another matter. Here quantity of output is essential. Speed in production is of the first importance. Beyond a rapid run over the typewritten manuscript for the correction of orthographical errors and punctuation, no revision should be necessary.

Apart from anything else, the writer who has to make a living from his pen, and whose contributions are restricted, no matter for what precise reason, to the journals where the rate of payment is low, cannot afford to spend too much time over revision. It boils down to this: if the writer, when once he has mastered the craft of confecting saleable manuscripts, cannot turn out a certain minimum amount of finished work per working day he had better give up journalism and try something else. Also it is not advisable to put a manuscript on one side for a few weeks and then give it a thorough revision. All revision should be done while the subject of the article, story, or book is red-hot in the writer's mind.

Perhaps the best form of revision is reading a manuscript aloud without an audience, making the final corrections during the course of the reading.

A MODERN FIELD

If the beginner can manage to break into it, there is no better thing in journalism than writing for the sports pages. Every daily and weekly paper, whether London or provincial, carries a sports section. In some papers it runs to four or five full pages; in most it gets a page at least. In many papers it ranks as one of the most important features.

It has a technique and a jargon of its own, but any competent journalist can master both in a matter of hours. The difficulty is not in the writing of sports articles – they are among the easiest things on earth to confect – it is in getting a foot into the field. Most of the stuff printed is staff work. True, there are a considerable number of articles printed over the names of famous footballers, cricketers, golfers, boxers; but all that these sports celebrities have written, in the huge majority of cases, is their names – the articles themselves are either wholly written by the staff or have received a good deal of attention from the re-write man. There may be, here and there, a famous boxer or a noted cricketer, who fancies he has a gift for writing and insists on having a hand in confecting the articles appearing over his signature. One can, on occasion, well understand that this has actually happened. For often they are terrible enough, these sports articles, God knows, for anyone to have written them!

Occasionally a champion gets the job of sports editor, but here again it does not follow that he does any actual writing. I believe it was Hearst in America who first realised the advertising value of a champion as a sports editor. He paid Sullivan a huge salary for doing nothing more than sit at a desk for a few hours a day. He paid Fitzsimmons $5,000 a year for the use of his signature. These experiments were successful, and champions in other sports were engaged at big figures to keep the boxers company.

There are, however, *some* opportunities for the free-lance. He will do well to try his hand on the provincial Press, which cannot afford to pay for big names. The pay for reports of local happenings will not amount to much, but there is always a possibility of such work leading to a staff appointment.

OBTAINING THE MATERIAL

A difficulty experienced by every beginner is that of securing the basic facts and data upon which he is to construct his articles.

To secure this data the free-lance journalist must keep his eyes and ears ever open, his imagination working overtime, and his note-book in constant use.

It is not enough to trust to one's memory alone. In this way a valuable idea is often lost. Whenever an idea for a new article strikes one, it should be jotted down in the note-book. An idea may come to one in a most unlikely spot, and at a most unexpected moment. It may be the result of one's observation when walking along the street; it may spring from the chance remark of a friend or an acquaintance with whom one is conversing in a pub or restaurant.

Every journalist should have a file of press-cuttings. The daily and weekly newspapers are mines of information and inspiration. Anything which is likely to be of use now or at some future time should be clipped out. It is not sufficient merely to clip out the slip and push it into a drawer or box. It must be filed for easy and rapid reference. No elaborate or expensive filing device is necessary. My own method is to use a number of large envelopes, such as I employ for sending out short manuscripts. These envelopes are marked with suitable headings, and all cuttings relating to a certain subject are pushed into the envelope bearing the appropriate subject heading. The envelopes are arranged in alphabetical order in a large drawer. With this system any number of additions are easily and quickly made, and out-of-date cuttings can be destroyed with a minimum amount of trouble. This press-cutting file represents one of the most useful tools a free-lance journalist can possible possess.

A few reference books are required. The following list should, in most cases, prove adequate.

The Writers' and Artists' Year Book.
Willing's Press Guide
Who's Who
Whitaker's Almanack
Fowler's A Dictionary of Modern English Usage
Roget's Thesaurus
A good encyclopaedia
A standard English dictionary
A dictionary of quotations

THE MARKET FOR POETRY:
VERSE AND ITS LIMITATIONS

Few poets, apart from those of world-wide fame, can make even a bare living from the sale of verse alone.

At certain times, such, for instance, as the outbreak of war, there is a demand for patriotic verse at remunerative rates, but in the ordinary way nobody is interested in poetry. There is no sale for it strictly as poetry. It is used, if at all, to fill up odd corners and fag ends of pages in the magazines and weekly newspapers. The pay, if there is any pay at all, is meagre.

A tremendous lot of poetry is written and a tremendous lot is published. It is published, for the most part, in volume form; often at the expense of the poet who has written it. For the most part it is pretty feeble stuff. The sales of these collations, ranging from slim booklets of a dozen pages or so to elaborately bound hefty volumes, are negligible.

I am told there is a market for humorous verse, that the humorous weeklies, from *Punch* downwards, are eager buyers. But obviously it is a decidedly limited market. One can count the number of humorous journals on the fingers of one hand: at their doors are persistently hammering some 10,000 poets.

It will be well to stick to old-fashioned poetry that rhymes. Leave the modern stuff, much of which is indistinguishable from prose, to the 'highbrow' writers. This kind of poetry has no commercial possibilities at all.

THE TECHNICAL ARTICLE

It is a firm conviction of mine, born of long and extended experience, that the *beginner's* best opportunity lies with the technical press. There are, in this country and in America, a large number of trade and technical publications, and the editors of many of them are keen buyers of articles dealing with their respective lines.

The trade Press offers excellent openings for the struggling free-lance who is prepared to make a specialized study of some subject or other. It offers more favourable opportunities than the general Press because the number of manuscripts submitted to a technical journal is a mere fraction of the number submitted to one of the national newspapers. And once the free-lance has proved that he possesses special qualifications for writing on a particular subject he will find a steady market for his work.

There is, of course, another side to the picture. In most cases the pay is not good – there is, for instance, no possibility of ever drawing those princely cheques which the contributor of head-line articles to the Sunday papers can expect.

Nor is there any prospect of ever flaring up overnight into glittering fame as a result of the publication of a sensational article. The best that can be hoped for is a small steady income, with possibly a slight chance of some day being offered a staff position.

The output must necessarily be a considerable one; and with the passing of each year the work becomes increasingly humdrum and laborious.

Writing for the trade Press calls for no fancywork. In fact, the degree of literary merit required is exceedingly low. The one essential is knowledge of the subject. Skill in writing is always subsidiary to this.

Obviously there is a technique required. Obviously, too, the style in which the newspaper article is written is not the most suitable style for presenting an article on steel constructional work, or a study of the latest developments in colour-printing, or a description of a new breed of rabbits.

Although fine writing is not essential and would indeed be largely wasted on the readers of trade publications, clearness of exposition and accuracy are of paramount importance, or should be. An involved clumsy style is very common.

Articles in technical papers are often atrociously written. Every rule of syntax is broken, wrong words are used, as often as not the writer says the exact opposite to what he intends to say. The reason for this is that the bulk of contributors to technical or trade journals have no knowledge of the technique of writing. The writer understands his subject and, with the average individual's confidence in his ability to write, he proceeds to put his ideas on to paper in the most ugly and terrible English that ever gets into print. The editor corrects the grosser errors, and no doubt groans over the task. At any rate, there is one individual who has groaned to some tune. That individual is myself. I have had the job of re-writing crude technical articles, and a terrible task I found it.

It is obvious, therefore, that the trained journalist, in writing for the technical Press, has an enormous advantage over the untrained: he can put the facts down in clear, bright and entertaining English. All he has to do in order to qualify for the job is to study his subject with some care, and master the few details of technique that apply specifically to the writing of the technical article.

In addition to the fact that writing for trade papers often provides a most welcome supplement to the free-lance journalist's income; it is excellent training for the beginner.

The chances of acceptance are greatly enhanced if the articles are accompanied with illustrations, which can be either photographs or drawings. These can usually be obtained from the publicity departments of the large trade organizations.

The beginner's best course is to procure a copy of each journal connected with the trade or hobby of which he has some knowledge. In this way he can usually discover whether or not the journal pays for contributions (some don't); and whether it is open to consider unsolicited manuscripts (some publish stuff written by their own staff only, and others commission everything they print). If there is nothing in the paper to indicate the editorial policy as regards these points, a tactfully worded inquiry (with a stamped, addressed envelope enclosed) will usually elicit the required information.

THE REAL ART OF SPECIALIZATION

It was at one time taken for granted that the true free-lance journalist could supply on demand an article on any and every subject conceivable. The tendency today is towards the opposite extreme. We live in an age of specialization.

Actually, so far as is concerned the necessary knowledge required for producing articles suitable for the requirements of the popular Press, a capable journalist can provide readable matter on any subject under the sun; and, from a newspaper point of view, he can present the superficial résumé (which is all that is usually required) more capably than can the expert on that subject who is *not a professional journalist*. The editor knows all this. But he has his public to think of.

This public has come to look with much suspicion on the jack of all trades. It is not impressed by an article on 'How to keep free from colds' by a writer who, a week before, was giving expert advice on exhibiting cats, and a month before that had his name appended to an article dealing with the trend of modern fiction. And, admittedly, there is a good deal to be said for this view.

If the beginner has out-of-the-ordinary knowledge relating to any particular subject or hobby, it will be well for him to specialize in that subject. If he can secure a reputation in this line he will find it much easier to place subsequent articles and, possibly, he may secure a share in any commissioned work that may be going. An editor likes to feel that he has a writer on his books to whom he can, with confidence and on the instant, apply for an article on a particular subject.

The great danger connected with specialization is the risk of a journalist getting written out. There is, too, that not-to-be-overlooked point that a specialist writer's output is necessarily restricted just as his market is restricted. Indeed, unless he can secure a commission to supply a regular weekly or monthly feature, it is almost impossible for him to make a living by his pen.

There is, however, a way out. One can, even in these days of specialization, write on many subjects. *The secret lies in being a 'specialist' on each subject.* It can be done and the public need be none the wiser. The way lies in the adoption of a different pseudonym for each subject dealt with.

5

PREPARATION OF THE MANUSCRIPT
AND FINDING A MARKET

ARRANGING THE MANUSCRIPT

Let us start at the beginning.

Your manuscript must be typewritten or produced on a near-letter-quality printer. Use good quality, A4 size, white paper

Double space the lines; that is, leave a blank line between each two lines of type.

Type on one side of the paper only.

Commence typewriting about 3cm from the top of the sheet. Leave the same amount of space at the bottom, with a 4cm margin on the left hand side. If you prefer to leave more space at the top and bottom, and a wider margin, do so; but there is no advantage in it, and you will waste a good deal of paper in a long manuscript.

Whatever margin you decide upon, stick to it. Set your machine and don't change it. Editors and publishers like uniformity in a manuscript.

At the top of the preliminary sheet type your name and address, and the number of words in the manuscript.

When the article is to appear under a *nom de plume* this should be typed in brackets after your own name in the top corner of the title page.

The calculation of the number of words is a simple matter if your margins and spacing are uniform throughout the manuscript. Editorially a word consists of six letters and a space. Count the number of letters and spaces to a line, divide by seven and you get the number of words per line. After counting the lines, to arrive at the number of words per page is a matter of simple arithmetic.

In the centre of the preliminary sheet the title of the article followed by your name or the pseudonym under which you wish it to appear should be typed.

Always make a duplicate copy of your manuscript. In nine cases out of ten, possibly in ninety-nine cases out of a hundred, you will not require it; but the hundredth time your manuscript is lost, or damaged, or destroyed.

Many amateurs have imposing note-paper printed with lists of all the papers and magazines to which they have contributed. This is largely a waste of money, because in most cases it is bad policy to send a covering letter with a manuscript. In the first place there is rarely any need for it, in the second place the editor will probably never so much as look at it. Very occasionally there are cases where a covering letter *is* advisable: in instance, where an article deals with a subject respecting which the writer has special or exclusive knowledge. And occasionally it is advisable to write a preliminary article suggesting an article. In the case of a writer who specializes on a certain subject, and does a good deal of this preliminary negotiating, I think the use of printed note-paper setting out the writer's qualifications and the journals to which he has contributed is advisable. But for the ordinary free-lance it can have small value.

It can, however, do no harm, and possibly may in some cases do good, to indicate on the title sheet of the manuscript any papers or magazines of standing to which you have contributed; thus, contributor to the *Daily Mail, Sunday Express.* But if your published work is restricted to verses or paragraphs in some local news-sheet, it will be far better to make no mention of it. One word of warning is necessary. The practice of adding under your name 'Author of *The Scarlet Clue, Literature and Life, et al.*,should be restricted to books or novels. Articles and short-stories should not be mentioned.

The sheets should be numbered consecutively, and may be fastened together in the top left-hand corner with a clip, or staple, or left unstapled. There are arguments for and against each of these methods. The clip is liable to slip off; the points of the staple are likely to rasp the editor's fingers or your own; if the sheets are left unsecured there is danger of some of them being lost. Of the three methods, I favour the clip for all manuscripts up to six or seven sheets; longer ones should, I think, be stapled.

Send the manuscript flat in a suitably large envelope and don't on any account roll it.

Don't send a faint copy to an editor. The probability is that it will not be read.

Never send out a dirty crumpled manuscript. If it is badly soiled, type it out afresh.

In the case of a manuscript running into some 8,000 to 10,000 words attach a stiffener, i.e., a sheet of thin cardboard the same size as the sheets, to the back of the manuscript, and use envelopes large enough to take the manuscript.

Unless you happen to know the editor intimately don't address your manuscript to him personally. Just address it to 'The Editor.'

With the manuscript always enclose a stamped addressed envelope for return in the event of rejection. See that the proper stamps are affixed to the return envelope – never insert them loose.

In sending manuscripts abroad the matter of return postage is something of a nuisance. One who sends manuscripts abroad in any quantity, should purchase stamps of the countries dealt with. One can usually obtain these from dealers in foreign stamps. Or they can be secured from any Post Office in the country concerned.

Don't bind the manuscript in a pink cover with red cord. Remember it is a manuscript not an *objet d'art.*

If your article is accepted, don't haggle about the price offered. Think yourself lucky to get any offer at all. When you have achieved some measure of fame is the time to start haggling.

Don't write an indignant letter to the editor if you find he has altered one of your pet sentences, or left out a paragraph altogether. He's doing his job.

Don't ask the editor why he has rejected your manuscript, or to suggest where or how it can be improved or made printable. Giving free instruction in the art of writing *isn't* his job.

If you get an article accepted don't bombard this particular editor with all the manuscripts you have had rejected by other papers during the past ten years.

Don't give up your profession or trade in order to go in for journalism as a whole-time job on the strength of having had half-a-dozen articles published.

SELLING THE MANUSCRIPT

It is one thing to write; it is another thing to sell what one has written.

The beginner must always remember that there are probably, at a modest estimate, and at any given moment, a minimum of 20,000 literary aspirants trying to find markets for their wares. Every year thousands of these aspirants, disappointed and disillusioned, give up the game in despair, but coincidentally thousands of newcomers take it up with enthusiasm, and thus there is never any diminution in the number of manuscripts submitted to editors and publishers. To the contrary, there is a steady increase in the number of aspirants and the resultant stream of manuscripts, partly through the increased number of young men and women turned out yearly by the schools and colleges devoted to higher learning, and partly because of the policy adopted by the Press of featuring articles by celebrities, society leaders and illiterates, thus suggesting to the public that writing for the papers is the easiest imaginable form of making money.

At the same time, the number of journals requiring matter is clearly a limited one: a pregnant and significant fact which seems to be largely overlooked. Every literary aspirant believes that among the shoals of manuscripts submitted to editors every day of every week there is an insufficient number which reach the standard of literary merit required to secure publication. It is, for the beginner confident in his own literary powers, a consoling thought. But it is a myth. True enough, the bulk of the manuscripts submitted are rubbish. Despite this, however, there is for the finding sufficient good-enough-for-publication stuff to fill, from cover to cover, every issue of each periodical twice over.

Because of all this, the mastery of the art of selling a manuscript is every bit as important as is the mastery of the technique of writing it.

First of all the beginner must get out of his head the idea of selling articles for large sums. Newspapers *do* pay big figures for articles – but not to beginners.

Luckily for the aspiring writer the majority of periodicals can't pay big prices for anything more than a fraction of the stuff they print. Many of them, indeed, cannot, or will not, pay more than hack rates. It is these papers which give the beginner his chance.

It is useless to sneer at low rates of pay. The beginner who refuses to accept payment at low rates, will probably never get into print at all.

Actually these tenth-rate periodicals, with their low rates of payment for outside contributions, are a god-send to the beginner. Here is a field where the competition of big names is not to be feared. Not that competition isn't fierce. It is. But the field is one where the beginner competes on terms of equality with his rivals.

A manuscript may be rejected for any one of a considerable number of reasons. The reason may have nothing whatever to do with literary merit. In fact, apart from the high-class reviews and a few magazines, literary merit has very little to do with either acceptances or rejections. The paper may be fully stocked with manuscripts for some time to come (a very frequent cause of rejection); the manuscript may be submitted at an inappropriate time; in the case of a topical article the subject may have ceased to be 'news' by the time the manuscript reaches the editor's desk; the subject may be one that is covered adequately by the staff.

Very often the manuscript is sent to a paper for which it is quite unsuitable. It is amazing how careless beginners are in this respect. It almost looks as if they took the names of the periodicals appearing in *The Writers' and Artists' Year Book seriatim* and addressed to each in turn, giving no consideration whatever to the requirements of these journals. Study the journal and its requirements before submitting any manuscripts.

THE VALUE OF PERSEVERANCE

One of the secrets of success in the profession of letters is perseverance. One must turn a frozen face to the disappointments resulting from the return of manuscript after manuscript, and the accumulation of a pile of rejection slips.

If it had not been for this perseverance, a huge number of famous writers would never have achieved success. Joseph Conrad worked at the craft on and off for twenty years before he landed a manuscript; W.L. George collected 721 rejection slips in three years. And there are others.

At the same time it must be admitted that there are thousands who have collected hundreds of rejection slips and that's all – there was no fame or fortune to complete the story, a point which writers of journalistic textbooks and advertisers of correspondence school courses omit to mention. Whether, had they persevered for another twenty years, they would eventually have succeeded is problematical – personally I gravely doubt it. *And certain it is that there is not room in journalism for all who aspire to it*. There must be a weeding out.

How long should one go on sending out a manuscript? Obviously there can be no hard and fast rule. The only safe rule to follow is to send it to every publication for which it seems suitable. I have had an article accepted after fifteen rejections; and there are no doubt many who can top my record. In fact, a writer in the United States some years ago mentioned having sold twelve stories each one of which had been rejected between forty and fifty times.

It is not advisable to build up hopes because a manuscript is retained for a long time. Editors vary tremendously in the time they take to consider manuscripts submitted to them. Some of the dailies return rejected contributions with a promptitude that causes many beginners to think their manuscripts have never been read; many of the weeklies keep them for months on end.

The question often arises as to how long an interval should one allow to elapse before inquiring about a manuscript, or whether one should inquire at all? It depends upon the nature of the manuscript in question. If it is a topical article, a tactfully worded inquiry should be made after a week has gone by. If on the other hand it is an article which is not likely to date, it is as well to forget all about it for two or three months and get on with some other work. There is always a possibility that an editor may be temporarily overstocked, but may be holding the manuscript over in the hope of being able to print it later – in such a case any premature inquiry on the part of the author will probably lead to the immediate return of the manuscript. There are limits to this waiting business, however, and when six months have gone to glory an inquiry should be made.

6

JOURNALISTIC SIDELINES

BOOK REVIEWING

Book reviewing is of two kinds: (1) literary criticism in the true sense of the term, where the book in question forms the theme of an article, and the critic uses it as a peg upon which to hang his own observations and reflections; and (2) bald, bare, short notices which are often mere synopses of the contents in the case of a non-fiction book and of the plot in a novel; and which strictly speaking, are not critiques at all but merely reports.

Reviews of the class (1) type are almost entirely confined to the high-class literary journals, and are usually though not always signed; those of class (2) type appear in many of the daily papers, the popular weeklies and the provincial Press, and are generally unsigned.

Literary criticism of the review-article type, especially in the form of the book page in a big popular newspaper, is often well-paid. But in the daily Press it is not so much the literary ability of the critic that is being paid for as his name – personality is of more importance than criticism, which may be weak.

The review-article, to be well done, calls for a wide knowledge of both classical and contemporary literature. In the case of a non-fiction book it calls for something more – it calls for some knowledge of the subject matter of the book in question. The inadequacy and the general vagueness of a review are often due more to the critic's lack of competence than to anything else. A review that does not attempt to value and to criticise the author's thesis, but contents itself with vague generalities about the style in which the book is written and congratulations about the paper, the binding and the adequacy of the index, is not a review at all – it is a bit of irritating clap trap. This manner of reviewing is extremely common. It is often adopted, as I say, because the critic is out of his depth and plainly incompetent to appraise the work in question. Again, in some instances, the book is never even read. The critic contents himself with a glance through the publisher's blurb, the introduction, and perhaps the final chapter. Often, owing to the number of books to be criticised and the limited amount of time available, with the best will in the world, it is a sheer impossibility for him to do more. This is the method usually adopted in respect of the books which get paragraphs varying in length from one line to fifty lines.

The aims of the true critic are to lay bare the author's object and to discover how thoroughly and competently he has proved or elucidated his particular thesis. The fact of whether or not the author's viewpoint is violently antagonistic to that of the critic is irrelevant. A prejudiced critic is a poor critic.

The terms destructive and constructive as applied to literary criticism are meaningless. Criticism, if it is worth the name, is constructive in its destructiveness, and destructive in its constructiveness. Most literary and dramatic critics are plainly incompetent: they betray their incompetence by praising everything outrageously; by writing those feeble, per-functory, inadequate notices that do not rank as valuations at all; or by condemning a book that has offended them by such trivialities as a couple of orthographical errors, a grammatical slip, a partiality for certain words, a peculiarity of style. This is not criticism; it is childish fault finding.

The trouble with the critic who praises extensively is that when a work of genius does happen to come along, he has nothing left with which to lift it out of the ruck. Most of the younger critics overdo it. It is, in fact, a feature of reviewing today that of the books noticed at all, ninety-nine per cent are eulogised out of all proportion to their merits. The author of a 'best-seller' is certain to receive adulatory notices of his future books from the critics – for some queer reason the average reviewer is averse to doing anything but praise the works of an author whose previous books have been praised either by other critics or by himself.

This attitude is one which plainly spells incompetence. The critic who is a true critic damns as readily as he praises. In this way, too, he becomes a personality.

So much for the art of literary criticism. Having mastered that art, or having an itch to become a reviewer, how does one set about getting books to review.

The difficulties in the way of an unknown writer securing an appointment as a book reviewer are enormous. Reviewers are divisable into two classes. There are those who write the book columns for the big dailies and the Sunday newspapers, such as the *Daily Mail*, the *Independent*, the *Observer*, the *Sunday Times*: without exception these are well-known writers. There are those who write the short notices in the weeklies and in the provincial papers: almost always are these reviews written by members of the staff. In some few cases the same critic writes both types of review. Actually, few reviews of any kind are the work of free-lance journalists. Occasionally, an editor may, in the case of an important book on an out-of-the-way subject, send it to a recognised authority for review. But it is rare. The whole truth is that, apart from a minority of exceptions, book reviews are not considered of any great importance in the average newspaper office.

There is only one road to the securing of a reviewing job worth having and that is success in another literary field, preferably as a novelist. It is but another proof of the truth of the old proverb: there's nothing succeeds like success.

ADVERTISING LITERATURE

Recent years have seen enormous strides in the development of the literature of publicity. By this I do not mean the writing of advertisements for the trade columns of the newspapers – this is a profession all on its own and is outside the scope of the average free-lance journalist. But there is a continually developing form of advertising in the literary columns that does not come within the province of the writer of advertising copy, but becomes a branch, and a singularly profitable branch at that, of journalism, providing (for there *is* a snag in the thing of course) the journalist can manage to get a job of supplying the matter.

The number of persons seeking free publicity in the Press, or paid-for publicity which appears to be free, in other words, publicity of an advertising nature, in the editorial columns, is enormous. There are the actors, the film stars, the cricketers, the tennis stars, the footballers, the boxers, the authors, the theologians, the politicians, and a hundred and one others, who bombard the Press with personal paragraphs. Everybody knows, or should know, about these. But there are other industrious and omnivorous seekers of publicity in the news columns of whom the public does *not* know – not yet, at any rate. These are the religious organizations; the societies for securing this and for preventing that; and the pooled trade organizations for inducing the public to eat certain foods and use certain articles. All these pursue their respective jobs with much subtlety and considerable skill.

Every newspaper office in London is bombarded with this publicity stuff. Much of it never gets into print. It is purely a question of news value. If the actress or the author happens to be news at the moment, the stuff, duly edited, goes in; if the personage doesn't happen to be news, the copy whatever it is goes into the waste basket. These personal paragraphs are rarely sent in to the Press by the individuals concerned: they are handled by what is called a publicity agent. It is his job to endeavour to keep his client or clients in the public eye. Usually the publicity agent is a competent journalist, and usually his job is a full time one.

Much the same applies to the articles advertising specific food and other products. In some cases, however, there are presented opportunities for free-lances to write articles of this nature. I know there are such opportunities because I have written many of these articles myself. The journalist may be commissioned, by the combine running the advertising campaign, to write a series of articles; or there may be an arrangement whereby for every article in which is mentioned the particular product concerned and for which he secures publication he is paid a fee by the combine. Both methods are common.

I have supplied articles on commission, and I have been paid a fee after publication for such articles as I have managed to place myself. Obviously I cannot state here the nature of the foodstuff advertised, but the payment was at a reasonable rate and the articles, all of which were of a simple nature so as to appeal to the populace, were quickly and easily written. To the journalist to whom the opportunity comes, or who can create the opportunity, the writing of this form of advertising literature proves a most profitable sideline.

Many of the leading industrial firms nowadays issue magazines at regular intervals – usually monthly or quarterly – which are known to the trade as 'house-organs.' These constitute good markets for the free-lance who can provide suitable 'copy.' The object of each of these magazines is, of course, to advertise the products of the particular firm responsible for its issue; and to this end the contents, while not constituting advertisements in the ordinary sense, must provide, either directly or indirectly, but in no sense crudely or blatantly, publicity material for the product concerned. The articles should be bright, entertaining, and racily written. Occasionally a short-story is featured. The rates of payment vary considerably.

Allied somewhat to these trade magazines are the brochures issued in such profusion by various business firms, travel companies, holiday resorts, and other undertakings. These range all the way from brief prospectuses, such as are issued by hotels and such establishments to 10,000 or even 20,000 word handbooks dealing with health and fitness, or cattle management, or baby-rearing, or house decoration, or cookery; and incidentally advertising the products of the firm responsible for their distribution. One has only to study the advertisements which mention that a free booklet will be sent on application, to realise the huge number and variety of these advertising brochures that are being written and distributed every year. Many of these booklets are written by trained journalists; others are the work of some member of the firm who fancies he has a *flair* for literature.

The problem arises of how is the beginner to set about securing work of this nature? There are two methods open to him.

Usually, these booklets, particularly those of an ambitious nature, are prepared by one of the numerous firms of advertising specialists. If the writer has specialized in a certain line, has written articles and books on the subject, it will pay him to approach one of these advertising agents, enclosing specimens of his published work. But if he is not thoroughly *au fait* with the thing, and can provide nothing in the way of evidence as to his skill and knowledge beyond his bare word, it will be waste of time and trouble. Naturally these agents require the writer of such a pamphlet to bring to the task a specialist's knowledge in addition to literary skill. My experience is they are most exacting in their demands, and are not prepared to commission work unless satisfied as to the writer's knowledge and capabilities. One can well understand this. Any ordinary hack-writing can be done efficiently by their own staff of advertisement writers.

All things considered, for the novice, the second course is the better one. He should find out the firms dealing in the particular line which he thinks he could handle adequately, who have not issued any advertising pamphlets, or whose publications are crude and betray an amateur's handiwork. There are many such. He should then approach these firms direct and lay his proposition before them. In nine cases the offer may, and probably will, be declined with thanks, but the tenth attempt may meet with success.

PART III

THE BIRTH OF A BOOK

7

WHAT SHALL I WRITE ABOUT?

NOT A TOM TIDDLER'S GROUND

Even in these days, when the most noteworthy thing about fame is its essential transcience, the profession of authorship has a fascination for the public excelled only by the fascination of the calling of the professional singer or the film or television star.

It is the ambition of every free-lance journalist to become a fully-fledged author, to be able to prance before his fellows as a confector of books. But, apart from those who are scribblers of sorts, it is apparently the ambition, this book-writing business, of every second person one meets who can boast of a secondary-school education; or who has won a prize for a school essay, or in a newspaper-letter contest, or a crossword puzzle competition; or who has decorated for a couple of years or so one of the colleges of Oxford or Cambridge. To be able to show his friends and acquaintances a bound volume of his work, to stop at a book-shop and gloat over a tome flaunting his gilt-lettered name on its covers, represent the culmination of an ambition which he pursues secretly with much diligence.

A huge number of these aspiring authors are not interested in free-lance journalism at all, not even as a stepping-stone to authorship. A big proportion of them are not dependent on writing for a living; they have no wish to sweat at the task of producing anonymous articles for the daily or weekly Press. Indeed I think it is a safe inference that the majority of those submitting book-length manuscripts to the publishing houses are without any extended experience in the craft of writing.

Whether the beginner's ambition is to secure publication for a novel or for a non-fiction book, it is an ambition not easy of realization. Because of the facts I have just noted, there are hundreds of thousands of people who are not only fired with this ambition but who are actively engaged in turning out manuscripts and bombarding the publishing offices with them. Of the manuscripts submitted for consideration not more than one per cent ever get into print. This, too, despite the facts that there are more publishers today than ever before, that 50,000 new books are published every year in the United Kingdom.

The reason for this phenomenally high proportion of rejected manuscripts calls for no diligent search. To write a book of any kind that is worth the reading is not easy. It is very emphatically no job for anyone who has never before written for publication. And the bulk of those for whom this book is primarily intended are in no position to pay a professional journalist or an author to re-write their manuscripts and put them into shape for publication.

In another section of this work I have mentioned the advisability of every one who wishes to write a book serving an apprenticeship in article writing. I repeat this advice, I say again that in comparison with writing a book of any description, the writing of an article is child's play; that, in comparison with producing a novel, the confecting of a short-story is a relatively simple affair; that to expect to be able to turn out the full-blown product before one has mastered the art of creating the infant article is foolish, and merely asking for trouble.

But sooner or later every writer's thoughts turn to the production of a book. It is inevitable.

Now the field open to the writer of the non-fiction book has always been an extensive one. To-day, owing to the wider interest taken by the public in so many departments of activity, it is more extensive than ever. One has only to glance through the current lists of the leading general publishers to realise what various types of non-fiction books are published. They range from cheap popular handbooks to expensive highly-technical manuals; from snappy, crisp biographies to abstruse studies of eminent literary notabilities.

It is easy, however, for the uninitiated to be led astray by a mere cursory examination of the books published. It is important to distinguish between those which are published because of their selling possibilities and those which are merely printed to satisfy the vanity of their authors. It is the inability to make this essential and important distinction which induces many a beginner to write a book which has not the slightest chance of acceptance by any publisher for publication at his own expense. Every year a considerable number of volumes are issued at the expense of their authors. The majority of these never sell more than a handful of copies. The reasons for this are many. A doctor, a lawyer, a teacher, a clergyman, *et al.*, pays for the publication of a book in order to add to his prestige in his profession. The question of whether or not the book sells is of little importance. Apart, however, from these purely technical works, there are other books which burst into print at the expense of their authors. Year after year, hundreds of these books are published, the majority of which are not worth reading. They are empty tomes, dull as ditch-water, platitudinous as a political speech. In the main, they consist of studies of long-dead celebrities – writers, politicians, theologians and the like. These puerile works are printed – they are never sold, they are never read, they never do a solitary crumb of good to anybody excepting the printers and binders. They merely add to the literary garbage which already piles mountains high in the big repositories of learning.

THE BOOK TO WRITE

In deciding what kind of book to write it is not so much a matter of choice as of necessity. The book to write is one dealing with the subject upon which the writer is a recognised authority, or which he understands thoroughly, or of which he has made a detailed study; always supposing, that is (1) there is a market for a book dealing with such a subject, and (2) that the subject has not been over-written. There are certain books, too, which, whatever the beginner's knowledge may be, should not be tackled by an unknown writer. It is not so much a question of whether or not one does possess knowledge of a subject, as a question of whether the public believes or can be induced to believe that one has that knowledge.

THE BIRTH OF A BOOK

It is almost impossible for an unknown writer to induce a publisher to handle a volume of essays. It requires the backing of a very well-known name to get a sale for such a book. Even then it may not prove a profitable venture – in many a case where a volume of literary essays by a well-known novelist appears its issue is against the judgment of the publisher and is probably undertaken to avoid the loss of the author.

Biographies and studies of dead and living celebrities are featured heavily in many publishers' lists. The field of biography is full of possibilities. But care in the selection of the celebrity to 'write up' is necessary.

There is an important distinction between the dead and the living, in that there are openings for biographies of living persons whose claims to distinction may be purely of ephemeral interest, such as film and television stars, sports stars, singers, *et al.*, in addition to those whose names will live in history. As regards those whose claims to fame are of purely transitory character, as in the case of a famous cricketer, or a celebrated film star, no penetrative analysis of character is required, and the beginner will find such a biography presents little difficulty in the writing. In strict truth, biographies of this stamp are little more than 'scissors-and-paste' compilations. There is, however, a good market for such books.

The biography of a statesman, or a novelist of distinction present greater difficulties. Publishers expect the writer of such a book either to have exceptional information on his subject, such for instance as applies in the case of a descendant, a relative, or a friend; or to be an author with an established reputation. This applies also in the case of a recently-deceased celebrity. Indeed, the majority of such books are commissioned.

The biographer of the living is hampered considerably in his treatment, and is compelled, in order to secure publication, to do a good deal of eulogising and white-washing of the celebrity concerned. It is usual, before publication, to submit the manuscript for this individual's approval. It is for this reason that biographies of living persons are usually singularly tame affairs.

Especially, therefore, do we find the 'best-selling' biographies of today among those of long-dead celebrities, the more so as the success of the modern biography rests largely upon the realistic treatment of its subject – a method quite inadmissible in the case of a living person. Indeed, it cannot be too strongly stressed that the old-fashioned biography, with its saccharine-coating of the subject's sins and its industrious cataloguing of his virtues, stands little chance of acceptance. Nor, as regards a celebrity of more than passing importance, or a study of a literary genius, is a mere 'scissors-and-paste' work enough. The subject must be approached from a new angle.

Autobiographies and memoirs are in a class to themselves – they do not really concern the average free-lance except indirectly. The majority of such books are the work of already famous or notorious personages. It is true that occasionally one comes across the memoirs of an unknown man or woman, such as a tramp or a criminal or an out-of-work, but they are comparatively rare. Where the free-lance does occasionally get an opportunity in this particular field, is in the writing up of a book of memoirs or an autobiography from notes and documents supplied. The majority of these social, political, theatrical, film, and sporting celebrities are quite incapable of writing such a book themselves, and are eager to secure the services of a professional writer. It is, of course, strictly anonymous work but it is not difficult. The usual procedure is payment of a lump sum on completion of the manuscript.

Books of travel are welcomed by publishers. If brightly written and suitably illustrated they often prove satisfactory sellers. But here we touch a class of book necessarily restricted to the few. Not many free-lances have the opportunities for travelling.

Poetry sells so badly that it is almost impossible to find a publisher who will handle it, and as a means of making money it may be dismissed altogether.

Works dealing with sociological, political and economic questions of the day often prove highly successful. The prizes fall to those writers who are quick to see the openings which present themselves. And, in all such cases, the great thing is to be first in the field. In this ability to seize quickly upon opportunities presented for books dealing with new phases of thought in many departments of activity lies the secret of success of the writer of non-fiction books.

There remain the technical and educational works. Here the range of subjects is very wide, from the popular pseudo-scientific books which can be written by the average free-lance who is prepared to give some time to a study of the subject; to abstruse works calling for the knowledge of the expert, and which obviously are outside the scope of most writers.

Books of both the types mentioned may turn out to be 'best-sellers.' There is, too, a great advantage attached to the technical work: its career is not measured by the space of a few months. Many bring in steady incomes for their authors over long stretches of years; and they need not necessarily come within the ranks of 'best-sellers' to do this; whereas twenty-five per cent of the novels which are printed are dead within six months of publication.

There is, however, the inevitable snag, and it is one to be kept well in mind by any writer who thinks of bombarding the publishers of technical books with his manuscripts. It is a line that is soon *worked out*. Suppose, for instance, you happen to have made a hobby of dog-breeding and have gained some reputation as an exhibitor. You can probably write a most interesting book on dogs, and equally probably you can induce a publisher to handle it. Its sale proves satisfactory, and you are encouraged to attempt a repetition of the performance. But naturally and inevitably there must come an end to it. One book on dogs, possibly two books on dogs, even at a pinch three books on dogs, with your reputation as a selling factor, may and probably will find purchasers, but a fourth and a fifth would almost certainly fall flat, for even if you have not exhausted your subject you will most certainly have exhausted your market. You cannot very well turn to cats or rabbits or poultry, unless you happen to have the requisite knowledge and are a recognised authority on these subjects as well, both of which suppositions are most unlikely. This is the trouble with all technical books – the author quickly exhausts himself. And so, to the professional writer, the purely technical handbook is at best merely a fill-up.

Educational works for schools and teachers are in a class to themselves. There is little scope here. Apart from the fact that no one outside the educational profession has any chance of getting a book of this kind published, the work is badly paid.

Books for teachers have small sales and usually involve heavy production costs. Usually they are written by college professors, or are theses for University degrees, and may be published at their authors' expense. Books for schools, owing to the low selling prices and relatively heavy cost of production, require huge sales to make them profitable. Finally, every teacher and University professor tries his or her hand at the game, and as a result the market is badly overcrowded.

HOW TO WRITE IT

Apart from poetry, volumes of reminiscences, and certain 'scissors-and-paste' compilations, the non-fiction book is more difficult to write than the average novel. Not only is the actual writing more difficult, but the labour of preparation is infinitely greater. This, of course, varies considerably according to the nature of the book in question, but a very high proportion of non-fiction books call for the expenditure of a good deal of time in research work. All things considered, the preparation and writing of a technical work involve as much labour as would suffice for the writing of two or three ordinary length novels.

There are other difficulties connected with the writing of a non-fiction book which are unknown to the confector of novels. A story, to a certain extent, tells itself. Once you have got the characters in action they help considerably in the unfolding of the story. In a non-fiction book this does not apply. There are no aids. It is a case of logical construction, careful planning out, the searching for and the elimination of material. It is extremely difficult to avoid repetition. So much so indeed that I am open to guarantee that no writer of a first book can avoid repeating himself at least once in the first fifty pages. It is true that in some books, especially those of an esoteric, involved or abstruse nature, a certain amount of repetition is advisable and may even be essential in order to get a point 'over,' but this is something quite different from carelessness in writing or revision – a fact which should be made sufficiently clear to the reader either by actual statement or by implication.

There is a prejudice against books which are short. It is not so much a question of value for money in this case, as it is with the novel; for the price of the book can be fixed in accordance with its size and cost of production. But for some unfathomable reason, reviewers as well as readers generally have got it into their heads that nothing worth saying can be said briefly. It is a fact that fat tomes invariably secure better reviews than do small books. Anything that does not exceed 25mm in thickness, that in page size is less than demy octavo, stands a singularly small chance of being reviewed at all.

Every writer of a non-fiction book other than an essay or a collection of poems, or an autobiography, is faced with the difficulty respecting quotations from other works. If he includes too many quotations, or decorates every other page with foot-notes, he is in danger of being accused of merely offering a 'scissors-and-paste' compilation: if, on the other hand, he makes no quotations or references he is pretty sure to be accused of presenting an unauthoritative and a badly-documented treatise. To decide how much to quote is therefore a matter of some niceness and, to a considerable extent, it depends on the kind of book in question. In a frankly technical work, the purely educational, and the biographical, it is well to provide plenty of references; in all other works the notes should be kept at a minimum. In all cases where actual quotations from the works of other writers are essential or advisable full acknowledgement of their sources must be given. In the case of long quotations the consent of the author or publisher to their reproduction must be secured. It is well to restrict the use of notes, as much as possible, to references to books and authors. Nothing tries the patience of a reader so much as explanatory passages stuck at the foot of the page – these should, wherever possible, be incorporated in the text.

Where it *is* necessary to include explanatory notes, as, for instance, often happens in the case of biographies and in scientific or technical works, it is preferable in every way to bunch these notes together at the end of the book, or, if preferred, at the end of each chapter. This does away with the irritation to the reader induced by the appearance of footnotes on every page, which in some instances that I have come across occupy more space than the text itself. At the same time

74

it satisfies those, and they are many, who require the fullest possible documentation for every statement.

Where the notes are purely references to books or journals it is advisable, especially if they are in any way numerous, to present them separately, marking each of these sheets at the top with the words 'Notes to Chapter X' circled in ink. All notes, and the references to the text appearing on one page, should be numbered consecutively, and not with stars and symbols. Where the notes appear collectively at the end of the book or of each chapter, they should be numbered consecutively throughout the book, or in each chapter, as the case may be. These note references to books and journals should give name of author; name of publication (in italics); volume number, if a book of more than one volume, or a journal; number of page referred to; publisher and place and year of publication.

Where quotations from other books or periodicals are included in the text, the beginner is often in doubt as to whether to include them in the body of the text or to make into separate indented paragraphs to appear in smaller type. My own plan is to place in quotes in the body of the text any extracts of forty words or under. Longer quotations are given in the form of separate indented paragraphs for setting in small type.

Care should be taken, where a quotation is made at all, that enough of the text is reproduced to give the author's full meaning. It is a practice with many writers, and a pernicious one which cannot be too greatly deplored, to pick out a sentence which, divorced from its context, supports the writer's thesis, whereas in its original setting it conveys a totally different meaning. In this connection the young writer should beware of quoting from an extract where he has not had recourse to the book from which the quotation has been taken. Many egregious errors have been made in this way.

When it is desired to omit a sentence or a few words from the body of the extract, or to start a quotation half way through a paragraph, such omissions should be indicated by a series of points, thus .... Any interjected comments of your own, either in the body of the extract or immediately following it, should be placed within square brackets, thus: [xxxx]

8

GETTING A BOOK PUBLISHED

PREPARING THE MANUSCRIPT

The methods which apply in the case of a short manuscript, as regards paper, typewriting and spacing, apply to the longer manuscript. (*See* Chapter 5).

Every chapter must commence on a fresh sheet.

The sheets should be of uniform size throughout. Where an insertion is made, always use the same sized sheet as the rest of the folios. Small sheets or slips are likely to be lost when the manuscript gets into the printer's hands.

Alterations to the typescript, if not too numerous, may be made in ink. It is not necessary to re-type a page of manuscript, because of two or three small alterations in the text. The publisher's reader is not prejudiced against a manuscript by a few alterations in ink; it is when errors, which have not been corrected, stare at him from the typescript that he is inclined to form a bad first impression of the work.

The sheets should be numbered consecutively throughout the book. If additional pages are inserted after the completion of the manuscript, these should be numbered and lettered thus: 47a, 47b, 47c and folio 47 should be marked 'Followed by 47a–c'. An omission is indicated on the sheet previous to the one omitted – thus if sheet 9 is taken out, sheet 8 is numbered 8–9.

On the outside sheet is given the title of the book, the author's name or *nom de plume*, whichever it is desired the book should be published under; and in the top or the bottom left-hand corner in type, the author's name and address. In the opposite corner it is advisable to state the approximate number (to the nearest thousand) of words contained in the manuscript.

After the covering sheet, the preliminary pages should be placed in the order in which they are to appear if ever the manuscript becomes a printed book. Thus:

(a) Half-title.
(b) List of books published by the author (if any).
(c) Title page.
(d) Copyright page and printers imprint.
(e) List of contents.
(f) Foreword or introduction by some authority or celebrity (if any).
(g) Preface or introduction by the author.

The back pages should be arranged in the following order:

(a) Notes (if any).
(b) Bibliography (if any).
(c) Glossary (if any).
(d) Index.

A page with the heading 'Index' should be included in the manuscript. This is merely to indicate that an index is to be included. Actually the index cannot be compiled until *after* the manuscript is in type and paged.

Nearly every non-fiction book is all the better for an index. There are exceptions, such as volumes of collected essays or other short pieces, where an index is unnecessary. Also very short books or pamphlets.

The manuscript should not be stitched together in one complete wad or have each chapter fastened together separately. It should be held together with a strong elastic band of appropriate size and it is a good idea to have a sheet of card on the bottom.

THE WEARY SEARCH

Now commences the most difficult task of all – getting the manuscript published. The search for a publisher is one of the most wearisome and disappointing tasks on earth. Moreover, it is necessarily a slow one. For it takes time to submit a lengthy manuscript to a number of publishing houses. One can rarely send out a full-length book to more than four or five publishing houses in six months, and many a manuscript has to make all these journeys, or more, before finding a resting place. Some publishers are so prompt that the author accuses them of never even reading his manuscript; others keep it for three to four months at a stretch, finally returning it with that most maddening of all missives the printed rejection slip. There are, of course, many variations. I have had a manuscript accepted for publication within ten days of its despatch; I have had one returned after having been under consideration for a full year.

It is well that the beginner should be under no illusion. It is exceedingly difficult to get a first book, unless it is of an exceptional nature, issued under the imprint of a reputable publishing house. I know there is a popular idea to the contrary; I know that in responsible journals, and from the pens of those who should know better, the idea is given currency that it is easy for a beginner to get into print. I have read till I am tired of reading that a well-written capable book is certain to find a publisher sooner or later; that a badly-written or poor book will never be accepted by any publisher. With all respect, I say stuff and nonsense! There are dozens of excellent manuscripts going the round at this moment that have not the smallest hope of ever being published for the simple but compelling reason that, despite their merit, they are not commercial propositions, they would not sell nearly enough copies to cover the costs of publication. There are hundreds of books published every year that are badly-written, but they happen to come within that queer category known as 'selling propositions,' they are printed because they possess that indescribable something which predisposes the publishers in their favour or ensures for them successful sales. And, in addition, there are, of course, the numerous books printed at the expense of their authors and issued by the 'vanity publishers.'

There are numerous cases where highly and sometimes sensationally successful books were rejected by publisher after publisher, and it is these instances that are eternally trotted out as providing proof that in the end a manuscript of merit is always discovered by some publisher or other. But is it? I gravely doubt the truth of this statement. What of the hundreds of cases where the manuscripts never do find acceptance; where each of the authors, after a dozen or more rejections, wearies of the task and destroys the manuscript? In many an instance it may be a work of great talent that is destroyed. On the other hand it may be, and in the huge majority of instances it undoubtedly is, a bundle of rubbish. We have no means of knowing. But I have an idea that many fine works have fed the flames. They are never heard of.

One can waste a lot of time in sending to the wrong publishers. It does not do to take the first firm that one happens to think of and post off the manuscript regardless of that particular firm's requirements. There are houses which handle almost every kind of literary ware, but the majority specialize along certain lines. In many cases they have special facilities for selling certain kinds of books. By a careful study of the lists of the various publishers a considerable amount of time and money can be saved. It would be worth investing in the *Directory of Publishing* published annually by Cassell and The Publishers Association. It lists every publisher and the subjects they specialise in.

Should the author approach the publisher before actually submitting his manuscript? The answer to this depends upon many things. In the case of a technical book, or indeed of any book which is likely to appeal to a restricted circle of readers only, it is advisable to approach the publisher first, as in this way much waste of time and postage can be avoided. Also where the author is uncertain whether the work deals with a subject that comes within the publisher's list. But in the case of *most* non-fiction works there is not the slightest need to make any such preliminary inquiry.

In the majority of cases it is sufficient to write a letter advising the despatch of the manuscript, mentioning the title, and drawing attention to any special points in connection with the work. But the letter should be brief.

The manuscript itself should be parcelled up carefully and substantially, sealed, and despatched per registered post, together with sufficient stamps to cover return registered postage.

I have already mentioned that publishers vary considerably in the time they take to arrive at a decision. There are many reasons for this. What bothers the young author is how long should he wait before reminding the publisher of the existence of the manuscript? He is anxious for a decision – naturally. He is wanting to get the book published at the earliest possible moment. Well, after seven or eight weeks have elapsed there can be no harm in writing a diplomatic note inquiring about the manuscript, mentioning its title and the date when it was despatched.

The majority of publishers have a stereotyped form of rejection. Some employ a printed slip; others write a formal note of rejection. The beginner is likely to write and ask the reason for rejection. It is inadvisable. Most publishers wisely refuse to give any reason.

Many beginners, though they chafe at the delay in returning their manuscripts, are indignant at what they are inclined to think is excessive promptness. If a manuscript running to 70,000 words is returned in two or three days the novice at the book-writing game is likely to jump to the conclusion that it has never been read. It is an unwise conclusion. Nor should the young author who, with suspicion big in him, sticks together pages 181 and 182 and finds them so fastened on the return of his manuscript, conclude that it has not been given proper consideration. He should remember that it is not necessary to read through the whole manuscript to come to a decision. In many cases not more than a score pages are actually read. But the decision is probably a careful and an adequate one just the same.

It is a debatable point whether, in selecting a publisher to approach, one should favour a small firm or a large one, a new firm or an old-established one? In dealing with a new firm there is always the possibility that the beginner's manuscript will secure more favourable attention than from a firm which has on its regular list a number of celebrated authors. Against this is the fact that a new firm may not have the selling organization that has the old-established house. This in itself is a most important factor. The beginner is likely to overlook it altogether. Not unnaturally, he thinks the big thing is to get his manuscript published – he has sufficient confidence in it

80

to imagine that once the thing is in print it is sure to sell. And in consequence, in ninety-nine out of a hundred cases, he gets the surprise of his life. It is not enough for the publisher to print copies, to send out a number to the Press for review, and then to sit down and wait for orders to roll in. There are publishers, true enough, who follow this procedure with exactness. They are bad publishers. The successful publisher has a selling organization and a publicity department of which the amateur author knows nothing. And that is why, to the author, the new publisher is always in the nature of a lottery. No author wants to have, if he can humanly avoid it, a failure. No publisher does either, for that matter, but a failure is a far more serious matter for the author than it is for the publisher. It is bad enough for an established author to have a failure; it is disastrous in the case of a beginner. It is terribly difficult to get a first book published; it is very nearly impossible to get a second published if the first has proved a failure.

Should the author employ a literary agent? The question has been debated a thousand times, but the answer is obvious to anyone acquainted with the craft of authorship. Bluntly stated, the facts are these. To a beginner an agent is usually of very little help. To an established author an agent may prove invaluable. Knowing the requirements of the various publishers, the agent is able to save the author a lot of wasted time in sending manuscripts to unlikely markets; he can often sell American, foreign, serial, film, and other rights. The beginner gains nothing by dealing with an agent who charges reading fees. His best plan is to submit his manuscript direct to the publisher – it will receive the same attention as it would if submitted through the hands of an agent.

TERMS OF PUBLICATION

There are four recognised methods of publication, two methods applying in cases where the publisher bears all the expenses of publication, and the other two where the author provides all or part of the costs of production.

(1) *Where the publisher bears all expenses.*

(a) *Outright sale of copyright.*

This is not exactly a satisfactory arrangement, and authors are continually warned against the sale of copyright. It is argued, and rightly, that if a book is worth publishing at all it is worth paying a royalty on.

All this is true enough, but the author is not always in a position to dictate as regards terms. It may be a case of selling the book outright or running the risk of keeping the manuscript in the drawer unprinted. In the case of the first work I ever wrote I sold the copyright outright – the book, which ran into several editions, was still selling thirty years later.

There is always the risk that the book may prove a 'best-seller.' In instance, *A Study in Scarlet*, the famous Sherlock Holmes story which Conan Doyle hawked all over London and finally sold outright for twenty-five pounds.

On the other hand, there are many cases where the author secures more money by an outright sale of copyright than he would have received in royalties. The book may prove a flat failure, in which case there would be little to draw in royalties even if the terms were of the most favourable brand. Indeed, in many a case where a book has been bought outright and proves a failure the publisher loses heavily, while the author scores. Also, in many royalty agreements, the first 500 copies sold are free of royalty, which means that a sale of 1,000 copies at £10.00. would produce £500 for the author. And it is the exception and not the rule for a first book to sell 1,000 copies.

In cases of pamphlets, juvenile books and many educational textbooks, the publisher often buys all rights. Also in some cases of commissioned books this plan is adopted.

(b) *Royalty Basis.*

Undoubtedly this is the fairest and the best method. The publisher takes all the risks, and pays the author an agreed royalty on the sales of all copies of the book (with in some cases the proviso that the first 250, 500, or 1,000 copies are free of royalty), ranging from about five per cent in the case of an unknown author to fifteen or twenty per cent where the author is already famous.

(2) *Where the author pays part of or all the costs of production.*

(a) *Commission System.*

This is the method adopted with theological, academic and other works where the author is more concerned with fame or kudos than with money. Large numbers of books published every year would not be considered by publishers on any other than commission terms. It is also the system adopted by the 'vanity' publishers.

The author bears the whole of the costs of production, and the publisher pays to the author the whole of the amount realised in sales less the cost of advertisements and an agreed commission for his services.

An alternative method is where the author pays a lump sum down as a contribution towards the cost of production, and receives a royalty ranging from twenty-five per cent to fifty per cent.

There is one writer of world-wide fame who published all his books on these terms. As an unknown writer he was compelled to adopt this method in order to get his early works published, so he carries out the same method now that he is famous and sure of huge sales. In such an instance, of course, the commission system is eminently favourable to the author.

(b) *Profit-sharing Method.*

This, the rarest of all methods, is most uncertain and generally unsatisfactory. It differs from the royalty arrangement in that whereas in most cases of a royalty the author gets a certain amount of revenue even where the book is actually a financial failure, in a profit-sharing method if the book is a failure the author gets nothing. On the other hand, if it turns out to be a 'best-seller' he does stand a chance of getting a bigger proportion of the profits.

A few points which the author should keep in mind, whatever precise method of publication is adopted, are:

(1) See that the date of publication is mentioned in the agreement.
(2) See that the price of the book is stated.
(3) Watch the Foreign rights.
(4) Don't overlook the possible value of the serial rights.

9

PROOF-READING AND INDEXING

THE ART OF CORRECTING PROOFS

After the acceptance of the manuscript by the publisher, and its setting up in type by the printer, proofs are usually submitted to the author for approval or correction. In some cases a set of galley slips is submitted in the first instance, followed by page proofs in the exact form in which they will appear in the book. Most publishers nowadays dispense with galley slips altogether, which they consider superfluous, causing an unnecessary expense and a certain amount of delay. Much time and expense can be spared if you have used a word processor and supplied the disc with the manuscript. It is worth asking the publisher if the disc will be used by the typesetter.

For some queer reason or other the majority of authors look upon the submission of proofs as an occasion for revising the whole book. They delete whole passages and substitute fresh ones, they make lengthy additions to the text. Even where these additions or substitutions are made to the galley slips they cause enough trouble and expense; where they are made on the page proofs the cost involved may be considerable. It is easy to see how this comes about. Suppose a line of type is deleted from page 15 and nothing is substituted, or suppose a line is added and there is no compensatory deletion: it means that every page has to be readjusted in turn until the end of the chapter is reached.

There should be no corrections necessary on the proofs, other than printer's errors. There is no reason in the world why a manuscript should not leave the author's hands in the exact form in which he requires it to be printed. If he has any doubts about it, the best thing to do, on acceptance by the publisher, is to ask for the return of the manuscript, and go through it again with meticulous care. If any alterations or substitutions *are* necessary on the page proofs, care should be taken, where the page concerned is any other than the final one in a chapter, to substitute the exact number of letters deleted or *vice versa*.

Many publishers include in their agreements a clause whereby corrections costing anything beyond a certain specified sum (usually 10% of the cost of typesetting) are chargeable to the author. This is to deter him from making extensive and quite unnecessary alterations and additions.

The proofs should be read *at least* twice: once for errors in spelling and once for the sense of the thing. It is impossible to combine the two in one operation. It is also, without long practice, exceedingly difficult to detect orthographical mistakes if the reading is done in the ordinary way. The sense of the passages must be destroyed if one is to spot every spelling error. The proof pages or slips should be read from the *bottom line upwards*, starting at the right-hand side of the page and taking each word separately. To prevent glancing at the previous line and thus getting the sense, it is advisable to take a blank sheet of paper and with this cover the upper part of the page or slip, leaving only the bottom line visible, and shifting the sheet of paper upwards a line at a time. By adopting this plan every spelling error can be located with ease.

The printers' marks that are in general use should be employed for indicating the necessary corrections, and not fancy methods of one's own. These marks and their use are shown in Appendix I.

Each correction should be made in the margin nearest the error. In no circumstances should an alteration or a correction be made in the text itself without any marginal indication.

Place inside a circle any instructions for the printer. The circle indicates that these are merely instructions and are not to be typeset.

If it is thought advisable, owing to the number of alterations or corrections, that another proof should be submitted, the word 'Revise' should be written prominently at the top of the page proof. List the pages you would like to see again on the first page.

Where there is a clause in the agreement that corrections other than printer's errors must be paid for by the author, it is well to use different coloured inks for marking the proofs; using red for the printer's errors and blue for any additions or alterations to the original manuscript.

Unevenness in the printing, and imperfectly formed letters, are often the result of the proofs being produced on a proofing system. These imperfections, which bother many authors unaccustomed to seeing proofs, and without any knowledge of printing, should be ignored. The publisher will see these faults are put right.

Any query on the proof sheets, whether made by the printer's reader or the publisher, should be given the most careful consideration, and a line should be put through the question mark to indicate that the matter has been dealt with.

COMPILING THE INDEX

All technical, scientific, sociological, historical, medical and philosophical books require indexing. The index is compiled from the page proofs. If done at all, it should be done thoroughly and carefully. A poor index is very little better than no index at all. It should not be too full, as in some books, featuring unimportant and slight references. It should not be bare, bald, and ambiguous, as so often happens – in many cases the index is of little more use than a list of contents.

In some books the index appears in two sections: (1) authors quoted, (2) subject index. In my opinion this division serves no useful purpose. On the other hand it wastes the reader's time and it is annoying. There is no reason why both authors and subjects should not be included in one general index. If it is thought advisable to differentiate between them, the names of authorities quoted or mentioned can be printed in bold type.

In compiling an index one of two methods is usually adopted. In the first method a large sheet of paper (foolscap) is used for each letter in the alphabet. This is the method I use myself. I start at the beginning of the book, and I write each reference on the sheet bearing its initial letter, followed by the number of the page on which it appears. When the whole book has been dealt with, each letter of the alphabet is taken separately and the entries applicable to it are again arranged in alphabetical order. This can be done by numbering them on the left-hand side of the sheet, or by cutting the sheet into strips and arranging the strips in their proper alphabetical order. The index can now be typewritten. In the second method, a separate card or slip of paper is used for every individual entry. When the whole book has been gone through and the references are complete, these cards or slips of paper are sorted into alphabetical order. If you have a personal computer with database or spreadsheet software, the task of alpha sorting is much easier.

The selection of headings under which to arrange the subject references calls for a little consideration. It is here that so many books are badly indexed. Often the reference is indexed under the wrong letter. A few examples will make this point clear. Suppose there is a page dealing with the evolution of man. It should not be indexed under the letter E – evolution of man, but under M – man, evolution of. Similarly the following misleading or useless entries are taken from actual indices:

Absence of maternal feelings *should be* Maternal feelings, absence of
Evolution of clothing *should be* Clothing, evolution of
Demeanour of lunatics *should be* Lunatics, demeanour of
Illusion of memory *should be* Memory, illusion of

Names of persons should be indexed under surnames thus: Carlyle, Thomas

Foreign names with prefixes, should be entered under their respective prefixes.

Title of books and newspapers should be printed in italics, the entry appearing under the letter of the first word in the title (except 'The' or 'A') thus:

Under W–*Woman in White, The*
"   B–*Bed of Roses, A*
"   T–*Truth about Psycho-analysis, The*
"   P–*Publishers' Circular, The*

Names of towns with the prefix St should appear under S. Thus: St Helens, St Annes

In titles of Saints, the prefix should be ignored, thus:

Under   P–Paul, St

"   A–Augustine, St

"   E–Eusebius, St

Where there are several entries under one general subject heading a dash should be used as a mark of repetition, thus:

Woman, emancipation of

—,   frigidity of

—,   inferiority of

although some publishers, to save space , will insist on running on, thus:

Woman, emancipation of 21,

    frigidity of 27, inferiority

    of 22

But where two similar words or names are repeated which are unrelated in their subject matter, the entry should appear in full in each case, thus:

Sex, determination of

Sex and its Mysteries

Three Soldiers

Three Weeks

A foreign compound name is entered under the first initial, thus:

Krafft-Ebing

Where the text relating to a specific subject covers or extends into several pages, this is indicated by the addition of *et seq.* after the number of the first page; thus:

Sun-bathing, benefits of, 218 *et seq.*

In any case where the reference is to something dealt with in a footnote, the indication reads

Sun-bathing, antiquity of, $97n$

In works of two or more volumes the complete index appears in the final volume of the series and the volume in which the reference appears is indicated by Roman numerals, thus:

Woman, emancipation of, II, 231

PROOF CORRECTION MARKS

The British Standards Institution recommends the use of proof reading marks that can be understood internationally. The full range can be obtained from BS 5261C:1976.

Marginal mark	Meaning	Corresponding mark in text
	Delete (take out)	Cross through
	Delete and close-up	Above and below letters to be taken out
	Leave as printed (when matter has been crossed out by mistake)	Under characters to remain
	Change to capital letters	Under letters or words altered
	Change to small capitals	Under letters or words altered
	Change capitals to lower case	Encircle letters to be altered
	Change to bold type	Under letters or words altered
	Change to bold italic type	Under letters or words altered
	Change to italics	Under letters or words altered
	Change to roman type	Encircle words to be altered
	(Wrong fount.) Replace by letter of correct fount	Encircle letter to be altered

Marginal mark	Meaning	Corresponding mark in text
↻	Invert type	Encircle letter to be altered
✕	Replace by similar but undamaged character or remove extraneous marks	Encircle letter to be altered
⌐	Insert (or substitute) superior figure or sign	/ or ⌃
⌐	Insert (or substitute) inferior figure or sign	/ or ⌃
⊢⊣	Insert (or substitute) hyphen	/ or ⌃
⊢⊣	Insert (or substitute) rule	/ or ⌃ (en or em etc.)
⊘	Insert (or substitute) solidus	/ or ⌃
⋯	Insert (or substitute) ellipsis	/ or ⌃
⌣	Insert (or substitute) leader dots	/ or ⌃
◡	Close-up — delete space	◡ Linking words or letters
Y	Insert space	/ or Y Between characters/words
Ⴟ	Make spacing equal	/ Between characters or words
�↑	Reduce space	/ or ↑ Between characters/words
⌐ or ⌐	Insert space between lines or paragraphs	
→ or ←	Reduce space between lines or paragraphs	
⌐⌐	Transpose	⌐⌐ Between letters or words, numbered when necessary
⌿	Transpose lines	⌿
[ ]	Place in centre of line	[ ] Around matter to be centred
(a) ⌐⌐ Move to (a) the left		(a) ⌐
(b) ⌐⌐ (b) the right		(b) ⌐

Marginal mark	Meaning	Corresponding mark in text
⌐	Begin a new paragraph	⌐ Before first word of new paragraph
⊋	No fresh paragraph here	⟿ Between pragraphs
⋏	(Caret mark.) Insert matter indicated in margin	⋏
᭞᭞᭞᭞	Insert single/double quotes	⋏ ⋏
⎯	Correct horizontal alignment	⎯ Single line above and ⎯ below misaligned matter
⌐⌐	Lower matter	⌐⌐ Over matter to be lowered; ↓ Under matter to be lowered
⊔⌐	Raise matter	↑ Over matter to be raised; ⊔⌐ Under matter to be raised
‖	Correct vertical alignment	‖
✕	Change damaged character(s)	Encircle character(s) to be changed
⊂	Indent	⊂
⊋	Cancel indent	⊢⊏
⊏	Take over character(s), word(s) or line to next line, column or page	⊏
⊐	Take back character(s)	⊐

APPENDIX II

AUTHORS AND THE LAW

THE QUESTION OF COPYRIGHT

The author's right in respect of all the products of his pen, published or unpublished, are governed by the Copyright Act of 1956. With certain exceptions, which do not concern us here, the author's rights under the Act extend during his lifetime and for fifty years after his death. He can assign to another party the whole or part of his copyright. The Act expressly states, however, that: 'no such assignment or grant shall be valid unless it is in writing signed by the owner of the right in respect of which the assignment or grant is made or by his duly authorized agent.'

Although this should be clear enough, there seems to be much confusion on the point. I have seen it stated on several occasions that unless the author of a manuscript specifically states the contrary, he is offering his entire copyright in the manuscript. This is quite wrong. In submitting a manuscript there is not the slightest need to make any reference whatever (unless in the case of a book which for some reason or other the author is desirous of selling for a lump sum down) to the question of copyright. Until he signs a document specifically assigning the copyright to someone else he is the sole owner of that copyright.

Similarly unless such documents have been signed in respect of short stories or articles published in periodicals for payment, they can be reprinted in book form at any time afterwards without obtaining permission from the editor or publisher of the journal in which they were originally printed. The act of asking for consent to their republication or the printing of any such acknowledgment is not necessary – it is merely an act of courtesy.

Infringement of copyright consists in publishing the whole or any part of a copyright work, published or unpublished, without the owner's permission. All quotations from the work of someone else are technically infringements of copyright. The fact that the source of a quotation is given does not affect the matter, the opinions of so many to the contrary notwithstanding. In practice, however, an author rarely objects to another writer making short quotations from his published works, as this is really a form of advertisement. But where such quotations run to anything more than, say, a hundred words, it is advisable to secure the consent of the author or the publisher, whoever is the owner of the copyright.

In the case of a review of a book this consent is not necessary. Extensive quotations may be made and the owner of the copyright has no redress unless it can be proved that such quotations are of such an extent or such a nature as to injure the sale of the book.

It should, however, always be kept in mind that infringement of copyright means the reproduction of the author's matter in the identical wording he himself has employed. It refers to the copying of words and not of ideas. There is no copyright in facts; where an infringement exists is in the duplicating of the author's method of stating those facts. Thus it is a common practice for one author to plagiarise the ideas of another author and present them in different terminology; it is common for a novelist or a dramatist to take a bit of that novel or play and another bit of this and weave these parts into a new whole. Shakespeare for one did this unblushingly and repeatedly.

These points should be kept well in mind and carefully considered by any writer who contemplates accusing another writer of plagiarism. Unless *proof* of deliberate infringement of copyright is of the clearest brand it is well to let the thing slide or approach the matter with caution. There is always the possibility that the accused party may succeed in establishing that the duplication was unwittingly done; or the further possibility that the plaintiff may be unable to prove the converse – in any case of this nature the onus of proof rests with the person

SUCCESSFUL WRITING

making the accusation. The possibility, too, of a counter charge of libel or slander is always to be considered.

The Copyright, Designs and Patents Act 1988 gives the author the right to be identified whenever the work or any adaptation is published. It is necessary for the author to assert the right in a contract, otherwise the right (of paternity, as it is called) cannot be infringed.

The subject of copyright is extremely complex and latest information will be found in *Writers' and Artists' Yearbook*.

LIBEL AND ITS DANGERS

Every author, except he be of the tame Sunday-school type of writer, goes about in dread fear of an action for libel. The more famous and the more successful he is the greater is the danger. It is this same fear of a libel action that haunts the newspaper editor, that gives him sleepless nights, that causes him to become painfully cautious in his references to any living persons, that make him scrutinise carefully every line of copy that goes into his paper.

The fact is that despite the greatest vigilance there is rarely a day passes than an editor does not publish something which may by someone or other be construed into a libel. It is rare that a novel is published that does not offer a similar opening.

It is only the dread of publicity that restrains many individuals who are injured, or who imagine themselves to be injured, from bringing actions at law. In this connection, it is worthy of note that sometimes a man is deliberately libelled for the sole purpose of tempting him to bring an action and so lay himself open to attack and exposure in a court of law. It was just such a procedure that Lord Queensberry employed in the case of Oscar Wilde.

There is an old newspaper maxim 'When in doubt leave out.' But this is largely an impracticable rule. At any rate it is impracticable in these modern days when no big national newspaper can hope to achieve any success without dealing with personalities rather than in bare facts.

Whenever a statement or an implication is made respecting a living person, it should be accorded the closest scrutiny and most careful consideration. Ridicule, abuse or attack in any form, is especially and invariably dangerous. Anything that is likely to injure, financially or morally, constitutes a libel, and the point so often brought forward that the statement in question is true, unless it is proved to be in the public interest and made without malice, does not affect the matter. Nor does innocence of intent to do any harm constitute a sufficient defence.

There is a popular notion that so long as names are avoided there can be no libel. This is not so. If it can be proved that the reference indicates the aggrieved person this is sufficient in itself to establish the libel.

The evil character of a person, or the fact of a conviction being on record, does not in any way justify the publication of reflections upon that individual's character or probity.

The possibility of danger in 'libelling' the dead must not be overlooked. Strictly speaking, there can be no such thing as libel of the dead, but if any of the deceased's relatives or descendants can prove that *they have suffered pain or injury* through the statements made, they have a case to put before a jury. Such cases are remarkably rare, but the possibility is one worth keeping well in mind.

Despite all the dangers and pitfalls it is possible for a provocative writer to attack mercilessly and ruthlessly, as that master of the art of abuse, T.W.H. Crosland, so clearly and ably demonstrated. In his own words:

'You must not reprove or expose him for the mere sake of reproving or exposing him and above all you must not bear malice. It is very seldom the attack which provokes a libel action. Ordinarily it is the reply to the attack ... out of sheer rage to accuse you of as many criminal offences as he can remember. And this is where the libel comes in.'